D0099723

DEEP

The Story of Skiing and the Future of Snow

DEEP

The Story of Skiing and the Future of Snow

PORTER FOX

Rink House Productions
Jackson Hole

www.protectourwinters.org

DEEP: The Story of Skiing and the Future of Snow/Porter Fox.

Includes bibliographic references.

Hardcover: ISBN# 978-0-9899732-0-5
Paperback: ISBN# 978-0-9899732-1-2

Cover Design: Basher Designs
Interior Design: Dammsavage Studio

For the skiers

Table of Contents

Acknowledgments   15
The Powder Life   17

PART I   **25**

The Road to Stevens   27
A Brief History   43
The Skiing Life   57
The Great Melt   71
The Man with Three First Names   85
The Signal and the Response   99
The Beginning   111
The Movement   123
On the Road   139

PART II   **159**

The Beast   177
A Castle of Many Rivers   189
La Meije   201
The Controlling Parameter   215
The Carbon Count   227
Energiewende   239
The Age of Humans   251
The Yellow Brick Road   265

Endnotes   277

Until one is committed, there is hesitancy, the chance to draw back, always ineffectiveness. Concerning all acts of initiative (and creation), there is one elementary truth, the ignorance of which kills countless ideas and splendid plans: that the moment one definitely commits oneself, then Providence moves too. All sorts of things occur to help one that would never otherwise have occurred. A whole stream of events issues from the decision, raising in one's favour all manner of unforeseen incidents and meetings and material assistance, which no man could have dreamt would have come his way. I learned a deep respect for one of Goethe's couplets:

Whatever you can do or dream you can, begin it.
Boldness has genius, power and magic in it!

—*W. H. Murray*, The Scottish Himalaya Expedition, *1951*

Acknowledgments

Before I start thanking, a few notes about the book. I used a mix of Celsius and Fahrenheit scales because we live in a world where both exist. When possible, I tried to keep measurements relative to the region being discussed. I used Chicago style throughout, but due to the amount of numbers in the book there are several exceptions for numerals, spacing, footnotes, etc. On skiing and snowboarding, the English language does not yet have a generic term for going downhill on skis, a snowboard, a snurfer or whatever. So I use the word skiing to refer to all downhill snow sports, under the assumption that we have moved beyond the whole snowboarder vs. skier nonsense...

There are too many people to thank for making this book happen. You all know who you are, and you have my eternal gratitude. Thanks to Ned Hutchinson and Steve Tatigian for getting the ball rolling—and to John Stifter, David Reddick and the extended *Powder* magazine family for their support throughout. Big thanks to Auden Schendler, Chris Steinkamp and Jeremy Jones at Protect Our Winters, in addition to Em-J Staples, Kim Stravers, Peter Kray, Ursula Damm, Jennifer Maravillas, Michael Coren and the Publet crew and the incredible photographers featured in the insert. Many thanks for insight and edits go to John Byorth, Christian Barter, Mark Kozak, Corey Milligan, Hal Thomson, Megan Michelson, Mark Moore, Richard Armstrong, Joel Martinez, Rob Castillo, Tiffany Abraham, The Paumgartens and Jeff Wogoman.

I'd also like to thank my parents for pushing me down the slope that first day and keeping me there until the closing bell against my will—and my late grandfather for encouraging me to avoid marked trails whenever possible. Finally, my everlasting gratitude goes to my wife, Sara, for her faith, guidance and companionship throughout this epic journey.

Introduction

The Powder Life

There is an island in Japan where, every winter, it snows 50 feet of the lightest powder on Earth. Two mountain ranges bifurcate the island, forming a four-pointed star. The Sea of Japan is 50 miles to the west; Russia's Kamchatka Peninsula is 1,000 miles northeast. When storms roll off the Siberian plains, they pick up moisture over the ocean and careen into the mountains. When settlers from the mainland arrived, they found men with bushy beards down to their waists living in homes with staircases that led to the second story—to skirt the apocalyptic snow that fell during the dark months.

Japanese emperors, soldiers and tourists started skiing Hokkaido's legendary featherweight powder in the early 1900s. It is important to qualify light here. The weight and consistency of snow is determined by its water content. You can make a snowball with one hand using 12 percent water-content snow. Alta, Utah—considered the powder capital of the U.S.—typically sees 8 percent powder, which blows off your sleeve like ashes. On the slopes of Hokkaido's peaks, water content is closer to 5 percent.

It takes a real powder hound to compare water content in snowfall around the world. But floating through "cold smoke" is a different sport than muscling through sun crust, sastrugi, boilerplate, death cookies, slush, corn, crud, graupel or even corduroy. A traditional ski turn on hardpack is initiated by angling, flexing and twisting. A powder turn is about balancing and leaning. It is not a battle with the hill; rather, it's a synchronization of your movement with the mountain's features—over and around rocks, through forests, down chutes and snowfields.

East Coast skiers hold a special appreciation for powder. I learned that as a kid in northern Maine. Between storms, the slopes were not icy. They were layered in the kind of black ice that you put in your drink. I didn't know any better, and as a teenager skiing symbolized independence to me more than sport. Every winter weekend, my friends and I loaded up a 1978 Peugeot sedan and fishtailed down Highway 95 to Route 201. We eventually slipped and slid up Highway 16 through Kingfield and Carrabassett Valley to the tiny cabin my parents rented for $500 a season.

What $500 a season got you in Maine in the 1980s was a roof over your head, four walls, two windows and 200 square feet of lime-green shag carpeting. My father added two couches, a coffee table, a military kerosene furnace from World War II, a toaster oven and a bag of lime to keep the outhouse somewhat civilized. After half a season, my parents never returned and the "Love Shack" became our personal theater—in which we acted out what we thought it was to be an adult. The shack was always the second stop on the trip, the first being Ayotte's Country Store, where we performed elaborate scenes to make us look old enough to buy beer, then handed the cashier a fake I.D. and three cases of Budweiser—a scenario that worked about half the time.

Sugarloaf still had some of its old magic then. In the 1960s and '70s it had become something of a national phenomenon, galvanized by a 1969 issue of *Playboy* magazine that called out the raucous wet T-shirt contests at the Red Stallion Saloon as one of the greatest parties in the world. Local Jud Strunk gave the valley its own celebrity when he became a regular on *Laugh-In* and appeared on *The Tonight Show Starring Johnny Carson*. By the time my friends and I started raising hell there, a new crop of bad actors, including ski filmmaker Greg Stump, were lighting up the trails and bars.

The concept of powder was vague to our crew then. We occasionally skied a few inches at a time, but always sank through to the boilerplate beneath. By the time I made my first trip out West, I was fixated on the fantasy of skiing cottony snow that didn't bruise my bones. My memories of that first trip to Colorado are a pastiche of snow, light, powder and wipeouts. My aunt and uncle lived in Denver and were excellent skiers. They let us warm up on a few groomed runs our first day before taking us to a powder field so perfect and pristine I remember thinking I'd skied it before in a dream. My uncle pushed off first, then my aunt and father. My mother, who had been a skier her entire life, wedeled through the field as smoothly as they did.

A vivid image of that slope is burned into my brain, mostly because I had no idea how to get down it. I couldn't see the tips of my skis or feel their edges touching anything. I remember my uncle telling me not to lean back, not to bounce down the hill. So I did the exact opposite and leaned back so far I could practically touch the slope with my elbows, bouncing through every turn in chaotic rapture.

My brother and I skied the run again and again, well after the rest of our group became bored and went off to another part of the mountain. The snow was soft and the turns effortless, especially once I got out of the backseat. The more laps we did, the more tracked the slope became, and for the first time I began coveting the little swaths of fresh powder that remained—and begrudged other skiers before and after us, speeding around them to get in another run before it was all gone.

By the time I arrived in Hokkaido 15 years later, a lot had changed. I'd gone to college, lived in Jackson Hole and gotten a job at *Powder* magazine. (Read Chapter 1 for the full story.) The through-line was always skiing, as it was the day the Japan Airlines 777 descended out of the clouds. *Powder* photo editor David Reddick and I spotted farms and two-lane roads crisscrossing the island. Forested hills ran beside and between them. The pitched roofs and cathedral barns at the end of each driveway looked like they had been transplanted from Wyoming.

A friend set us up with a rental car and pre-programmed the GPS to deliver us to a ski resort called Niseko. The voice guidance spoke Japanese, so we listened to the strange language over the car's speakers for hours, weaving between mountains and lakes and forests so thick you couldn't see 10 feet into them. Eventually the road climbed across a narrow bridge into the sheer folds of the Japanese Alps. It was dark and snowing hard when we finally reached Niseko. We dropped off our bags and noticed the bright glow of night-skiing lights on the hill. We hadn't slept in 20 hours, but after a few pulls of Japanese whiskey, we decided what the hell, we might as well get to work.

Murky light spilled through a sluice in the trees on our first chairlift ride up. The snowdrifts on the sides of the trails were four feet deep. Someone in line said that it'd been snowing for 10 days. Beneath the chair, gangs of teenage skiers and snowboarders bobbed to American hip-hop blasting from speakers mounted to the lift towers.

We found a wooded bowl off the top of the chair. The lights made the slope look green. Visibility was decent. Three tracks led to the 600-foot face below. I pushed off and felt my skis lift as I gained speed. I could hear the snow hiss under my bases and see a faint green cloud following David down the hill. The scene was like the recurring dream I've had every September since I was a kid. In it I ski down a snowfield, fly off a jump and never come down.

I skied between two birches and followed a skinny slot through the trees. A ridge cut across the slope about halfway down, and I hit it with speed. I don't know how far I went or how long I was in the air. The snow was so soft and light, I couldn't tell when my skis took off or when they touched again. It was not a short amount of time. It felt like hours in my mind. In that moment, I both remembered and realized the magic of skiing powder. It is the feeling of nothing. No resistance, gravity, distraction or consequence. Like that first powder run I had in Colorado, this was pure flight and the most transcendent and vital sensation I've ever experienced.

It is also why I wrote this book.

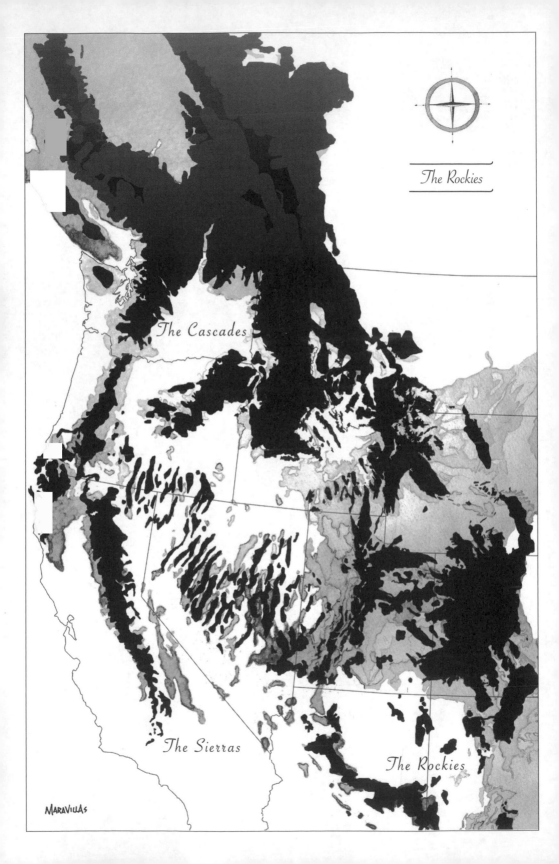

The Rockies

The Cascades

The Sierras

The Rockies

MARAVILLAS

PART I

Chapter One

The Road to Stevens

To those who have struggled with them, the mountains reveal beauties that they will not disclose to those who make no effort. That is the reward the mountains give to effort. And it is because they have so much to give and give it so lavishly to those who will wrestle with them that men love the mountains and go back to them again and again. The mountains reserve their choice gifts for those who stand upon their summits.

—*Sir Francis Younghusband*

All night, the snow came down. It fell at a rate of an inch an hour as a low-pressure system hurtling off of the Pacific slammed into the sheer ridgelines of the North Cascades. Earlier that day, the storm had buffeted the Washington coast with rain, thick bands of it falling from the dockyards of Seattle to the Cascadian gateway towns of Monroe and Sultan. When the clouds lifted over the foothills around Gold Bar, moisture crystalized into snowflakes and Stevens Pass Ski Area, set in the heart of the North Cascades 80 miles east of Seattle, took the full brunt of the most epic blizzard of the season.

The flakes fell sideways, straight down, in spirals and sometimes seemingly up. Their spiny fibrils clung to cars, signs, trees and the ski area's slopes, obscuring lift towers and the monolithic stands of old-growth spruce that divided the trails. Locals who understood the potential of a full-blown Cascadian whiteout salted their driveways and put chains on their tires. Seattle skiers who tracked weather on their work computers in the winter loaded up their cars and made a beeline for the high country the instant they punched out. After two weeks of no snow—and a winter that saw the third-lowest snow cover in the Lower 48 in recorded history—the night of February 18, 2012, was a dream turned reality.

That night, in the corner of the Stevens Pass RV lot, a small fire burned at the foot of a two-story snowbank. Washington ski resorts are unique in that they allow campers to spend the night in designated lots, and that night the RV lot was full. Stevens Pass locals deck out their campers with stereos, sleeping bags, ski-tuning benches and drying racks—creating the ultimate ski-in/ski-out headquarters. When the lifts shut down on February 18, the lot transformed into a pseudo block party.

Tim Wangen was parked in a prime corner spot and had hosted people all day in his RV. The 53-year-old lives nearby in a cabin on Lake Wenatchee and has skied Stevens Pass for more than 40 years. He knows the ins and outs of the resort, the mountain and the immense backcountry surrounding it. As friends spilled out of the Foggy Goggle bar and gathered around the campfire he'd built near his RV, he played ski movies on a flat-screen TV and swapped stories about the old days.

The bizarre 2011–2012 winter had been the fourth warmest in recorded history and had many wondering if climate change was to blame. Storms had been surprisingly prolific in the Northwest, though, dropping more than 40 feet of snow on the North Cascades. (Squaw Valley, California, had grass growing on its slopes in January.) More than a foot of new snow piled up on the RVs that day—all parked in a long row at a 30-degree angle to the curb. Dim light from battery-powered lamps and candles shone from the vehicles' windows, and the on-slope halogens from Stevens' night-skiing operation gave the lot an eerie golden glow. Another foot and a half of snow was predicted by morning, setting up February 19 to be one of the deepest days of the season.

A group cloaked in puffy down jackets, mittens and wooly hats collected around Wangen's fire and did what most skiers would the night before a powder session: they drank beer and talked about the mountains, work and their good fortune that a classic North Cascades whopper was descending on their favorite resort. The group at Stevens that weekend—some around the fire, others already home in bed—was unusual in that it included some of the best and most influential skiers in America. A few worked in the industry; others were friends tagging along. *Powder* magazine editor John Stifter and photographer (and former *Powder* editor) Keith Carlsen were there, as were ESPN.com freeskiing editor Megan Michelson and her fiancé, Dan Abrams, founder of Flylow ski wear. Professional skier Elyse Saugstad and Salomon Sports sales rep Joel Hammond had made the trek to the Cascades, along with Jim Jack—head judge of the Freeskiing World Tour (FWT) and a skiing legend in his own right. Chris Rudolph, the animated and much-loved 30-year-old marketing director of Stevens Pass, was the catalyst for the convergence. He co-hosted a Salomon promotional event that weekend and had been courting many in the group to come to Stevens for years.

Forty-six-year-old Jack rolled into the RV lot the night before with his 1971 Vacationeer camper attached to the bed of his truck. He was a Washington native and led Stifter and Carlsen to Wangen's RV that day after skiing. Jack first hit the slopes when he was five years old and had bird-dogged fresh powder and skiing jobs around the world ever since. He was a "freeskier" at heart, the definition of which has changed as much as skiing has over the last 20 years. To most, freeskiing means exactly what it sounds like: the act of skiing, free of racecourses, conventional trails and anything that smacks of tradition. It is everything that Olympic ski racing and sanctioned freestyle competitions are not—and includes halfpipes, BMX-esque skiercross races, creative big-air jumps in terrain parks and "big mountain" Alaska-style skiing, where skiers carve high-speed turns and land freestyle jumps on backcountry peaks.

The movement began in the late '80s and carried with it a renaissance in ski design and technique that took the sport to an almost supernatural state, with athletes flying off 200-foot cliffs and gliding down previously unskiable mountainsides in a matter of seconds. Jack's life and soul were deeply entwined with the sport, and he had become a kind of father figure in it, earning him the nickname "The Grandfather of Freeskiing" from the kids he coached on the FWT junior circuit. He was a masterful skier himself. People said he skied like he walked, which was smoothly and unhurried. When he was anxious, he went skiing. When he was happy, he went skiing. When he skied, he spontaneously broke out in laughter, the joy of it overwhelming even after thousands of days on the hill.

Jack stood by the fire, near the door to Wangen's RV. His life partner, Tiffany Abraham, stood to his right, her down hood cinched around her face, ski pants still on, arm around the man she'd lived with, road-tripped with and skied with for almost a decade. Abraham was a soul skier as well, a 29-year-old Stevens local who worked on the FWT with Jack and skied every day she could. She hung paper snowflakes in her house and kept them up year-round. Leavenworth, the Bavarian-themed town at the eastern foot of the pass where Tiffany grew up and where she and Jack lived, was known to skiers as "Never-Never Land." Jack was dubbed "Peter Pan" and Abraham "Tinker Bell"—because she took care of the Lost Boys of Stevens Pass.

Small ski areas are tight-knit in the way that small towns are: everyone pretty much knows everyone else. Johnny Brenan, a local contractor, was a good friend of Jack's and was parked close to Wangen's camper. Brenan had recently bought a new RV to take to Stevens, and his two daughters—hard-charging young skiers themselves—and wife were sleeping there that night. Rudolph had been with the crew earlier, but drove home to his bungalow in Leavenworth to be with his girlfriend. Stifter and Carlsen were at Stevens to cover a story on night skiing for *Powder*, and as the fire burned down, Carlsen climbed onto the snowbank and took photos of the scene.

Jack joked with Abraham that they better get into the shot, because who knew where the picture might be published. He'd shown Carlsen and Stifter, along with Brenan, the snow-filled glades of Big Chief Mountain all day. With an average of more than 450 inches of snow a year at Stevens, the funky 75-year-old resort was a secret powder stash for Northwesterners.

When the fire burned down, the group made plans to meet the next day. Jack and Abraham waded through the new snow to the Vacationeer—where they'd spent so many nights on the road together, they'd taped roadmaps above the bed to plot their next route. Wangen and the other campers climbed into their respective vehicles and Carlsen and Stifter made their way to Kehr's Cabin—an old lift shack refitted as a guest cabin that Rudolph had reserved for them.

By the time Stifter and Carlsen made it to the door of the cabin, the roof was covered in a thick white blanket. After skiing on ice and grass for most of the season in snow-starved California and Colorado, that day had been the best of the winter. And with snow still spiraling down, it looked like the next would be the kind most skiers live their lives for. The two hung up their jackets and made their way to bed. As everyone on the mountain drifted off to sleep, no one considered that February 19 would end in every skier's worst nightmare.

The skiing cosmos is difficult to explain to anyone not immersed in it. The act of skiing differs from traditional sports in that unlike basketball, biking or football, it requires specific orographic and meteorological phenomena. Because skiers depend on planetary forces much larger than themselves—and, like surfers, must work in harmony with them—a kind of otherworldly euphoria overtakes them when they do it well.

The sport also comes with a distinct lifestyle: ski sweaters, A-frames, Bavarian *Lüftlmalerei* frescoes, goggle tans and après-ski cocktails. Skiers don't ski the way soccer players play soccer. Serious skiers live, wear, think and talk about the sport almost every day, winter and summer—dreaming about it, reading about it, building houses to be closer to it and traveling around the world to practice it. The deeper they follow the rabbit hole, the more they identify with the sport. At parties they introduce themselves as skiers, and at work they check plane tickets, ski reviews and snow depths at their favorite resorts. A significant portion of college students throw away years of tuition every December to serve beers and pizza in a ski town and stand in line at 6:00 a.m. to get first tracks on the mountain.

They are not all rich kids, as many non-skiers assume. Modern skiing began as a pastime of the leisure class, and the early days of Mascara

Mountain (Sugarbush), Aspen and Mammoth—where movie stars and businessmen schussed with European instructors—cemented that image in the 1950s and '60s. But since the ski-bum movement caught hold 40 years ago, a good number of lifetime skiers are working-class folk who hold a job five days a week and ski mornings, lunch breaks and on the weekends. Of the seven million skiers in America, perhaps a half-million settle down in the mountains and dedicate their lives to the sport. For them, skiing becomes synonymous with living, the very act a metaphorical breath after a long week of work.

There are ski bums on Thompson Pass near Valdez, Alaska, who sleep in snow caves to save money for a helicopter ride into the Chugach Mountains and a 4,000-vertical-foot, thigh-deep powder run. There are others in Chamonix, France, who scale vertical rock and ice with skis on their backs to descend hardpack couloirs so steep they brush the snow with their uphill elbow every turn. Ski bums in Hokkaido, Japan, live in shame for turning their backs on the capitalist system and instead hole up in hand-hewn cabins on the flanks of the Japanese Alps—where it can snow 10 feet in a week. Across the Sea of Japan, Russian ski bums commandeer decommissioned Mi-8 military helicopters and fly to the 15,000-foot peaks of the Kamchatka Peninsula, where they ski five-mile runs straight to the ocean.

The sensation of giving yourself over to gravity catalyzes the addiction. Pushing off down a slope and feeling your body accelerate is mystical business, felt only by surfers, skydivers, bikers and anyone who practices a sport in which you go down. A century ago, the vectors involved in a ski turn were considered the bailiwick of gods or machines. In fact, the first American downhill racers—who hit speeds of more than 80 miles an hour during the 1860s in the Sierra Nevada—were the first humans to go that fast and live to tell about it. The sport cheats gravity and death and, in many senses, rationality, as skiers toe the line between control and chaos. To those who master it an epic run is a transcendent journey, until the grade evens out and you slide to a stop.

I have known moments like this in nearly 40 years of skiing, and it seems appropriate to relate some of them here so you know where all of this is coming from. I learned to ski in Maine when I was two years old, and by the time I was in high school I had thumbtacked ski-magazine posters to my bedroom walls—and performed a daily regimen of awkward exercises that were supposed to make me a better skier. I drove three hours to Sugarloaf Mountain Resort most winter weekends of high school, sometimes just for the day when school was closed for a blizzard. We caromed off refrigerator-size moguls almost exclusively during those years, then hiked into the 1,500-foot mountains on Mount Desert Island, where I lived, to leap off cliffs like they did in ski movies. We watched all of Greg Stump's films and followed young racers at Sugarloaf's Carrabassett Valley Academy, where Bode Miller trained, longing to emulate their form and style. In the spring, we made our way to Tuckerman Ravine in New Hampshire's White Mountains to give real backcountry steeps a try.

I chose a college in Vermont because it had its own ski hill and was an hour drive from a half dozen others. I worked on the college's ski patrol two days a week and skied most days when I was off-duty. When students headed home for Christmas my senior year, I stayed in one of the old clapboard houses near the little cabin where Robert Frost wrote about falling snow. My friends and I drank growlers of Otter Creek ale at night and worked for the patrol for time-and-a-half during the day. Two months later, eight of us drove two station wagons out West to find a ski town to move to when we graduated. It snowed two feet while we were in Jackson Hole, and the following fall we rented a townhouse there and moved into our first home together.

We followed snow through the seasons, learning to ski again on the steep couloirs and cirques of Jackson Hole Mountain Resort, training as river guides on the Snake River in the spring and hunting grouse in the Bridger-Teton National Forest when the first flakes came down in September. From there, our story follows that of many who choose the mountains over a career. We slept two to a room, ate unhealthy amounts of ramen noodles and cold pizza, paid the rent with credit-card checks and waited in line sometimes four to five hours before the lifts opened to get first tracks. Avalanches took several lives every year and we took a course to learn how to avoid them and how to dig each other out if we were caught in one. Ski-film production company Teton Gravity Research was just getting started in Jackson then, and we watched in wonder as skiers like Jason Tattersall, Dean Conway and the Zell brothers launched 50-foot cliffs into pillows of fresh powder and flashed thousand-foot lines in three turns.

I took a job at the *Jackson Hole News* as the sports editor and education reporter in 1995. (For $16,500 a year.) When I wasn't covering school-board meetings or junior varsity girls' volleyball games, I submitted stories about Jackson skiers like Doug Coombs to *Powder*. A few years after that, Keith Carlsen, then-editor of *Powder*, asked me to work at the magazine, which I have been doing ever since.

The *Powder* gig allowed me to ski on five continents, vanish into neck-deep powder in Japan, walk through Istanbul with ski boots around my neck and spend the night on mountainsides so remote I couldn't see a single light except for the spray of stars overhead. I walked to the headwaters of India's holy Yamuna River at 18,000 feet to ski down the snowfields that fed it; was introduced to aliens on the flanks of Mount Shasta by a spiritual guide before climbing and skiing the spectral peak; guarded a high-alpine ski camp in Bolivia with a Luger pistol as our guide walked to a nearby farm to butcher a goat for dinner; and hiked with skis on my back through valleys in Peru once held by the Shining Path—to ski 20,000-foot mountains, up which I had to take three breaths for every step.

What I noticed on those travels more than anything was a brotherhood in the sport that extends far beyond the borders of North America. I've seen *Powder* posters hanging on a travel agent's wall in the Himachal Himalayas and drove to a post-Soviet powder stash in Bulgaria with a gang of ski bums—in a wooden Moskvitch sedan their parents received 10 years after they ordered it in the 1970s. A few years ago, I climbed and skied a 13,671-foot mountain in Morocco over a week with a man who didn't speak a word of English. You don't need words when you are with another skier.

Skiing itself is your passport, language and kinship. Tell someone you are an American in most mountain ranges in the world and you'll get a mixed, sometimes chilly, response. Say you're a skier and you'll be taken in every time. The smaller the town and the higher the mountain, the stronger the brotherhood grows. It is an unspoken code, a natural and mutual respect skiers and alpinists afford one another. In the mountains and hamlets of the Pacific Northwest, it is something that binds entire communities together.

Most of the visitors who met up with Chris Rudolph to ski on February 19 followed the route Seattle skiers drive when the snow flies. The path from metropolis to mountain begins east of the mirrored skyscrapers of downtown, the red cranes of Seattle Port and the teaming fish markets spanning Pike Place. It follows State Route 520 past the bungalows and Tudor homes of the Montlake neighborhood and crosses Evergreen Point Floating Bridge—putting drivers at eye level, for two full minutes, with sailboats, seaplanes and ferries—before cutting into the forested shores of Lake Washington. Softwood hems the coastline there. Clusters of beech and maple stand out in the fall, a red-and-yellow smear across the constant green.

Route 522 continues over the aqua-green water of the Skykomish River to the old railroad town of Monroe, then connects to a road with near-mythical status to powder lovers: Highway 2, the Stevens Pass Highway. The road is no longer a road at that point. It's an existential link between life and living—life taking place in homes, high-rises, cubicles and coffee shops; living going down in the scene that comes into view a few miles down the road: thin granite spires, rockbound gullies and whipsaw ridgelines cutting across the sky.

Of all the skiing ranges in North America, the North Cascades stand alone for several reasons. The 150-mile-long subrange comprises the northern backbone of the American Cordillera—a 12,000-mile chain of mountains stretching from Tierra del Fuego to Alaska. The Cordillera forms the eastern edge of the Pacific Ring of Fire and, in the Pacific

Northwest, contains the only active volcanoes in the Lower 48. Rocks in the range are 400 million years old and have almost a dozen different crust samples in them, from volcanic island arcs to deep ocean sediments to chunks of subcrustal mantle. The diversity reflects the violent forces that formed the mountains eight million years ago—the result of a slow subduction of the Pacific crust beneath the continental shelf.

The North Cascades attract skiers for two distinct reasons. First, they plummet almost to sea level, giving them some of the steepest and longest vertical drop on the continent. Second, because of their proximity to the ocean, they are the first vertical landmass that moisture-rich storms spinning off the Pacific hit. The range receives as much as 160 inches of water a year on its western flanks, compared to 10 to 20 inches on the eastern side. In the peaks and valleys in between lies one of the snowiest places on Earth.

Blizzards in the North Cascades are unlike any in North America. When they hit, they come in white sheets, giant flakes accumulating at upward of three inches an hour. Snow events typically arrive with upsloping winds and temperatures close to freezing, creating a sticky, heavy snowpack. For skiers, the sheer amount of snow that falls makes up for the lack of lightness. Mount Baker, 80 miles north of Seattle, broke the world record for the most snow in one season during the winter of 1998–1999, with 1,140 inches. The previous record holder was Mount Rainier, 80 miles to the southeast, with 1,120 inches—all of which explains why Seattle outdoorsmen Don Adams and Bruce Kehr set their eyes on Stevens Pass in the 1930s as a possible ski area.

With the help of the Wenatchee Ski Club, the two cleared a run on 5,862-foot Big Chief Mountain, then convinced Franklin D. Roosevelt's Civilian Conservation Corps to construct a lodge at the base. Stevens Pass ski area opened in the winter of 1938. The sole lift was a rope tow powered by an eight-cylinder Ford engine. To get to the hill, skiers had to buy an 18-cent, one-way ticket through the Cascade Tunnel on the Great Northern passenger train, then take a school bus to the lodge. Since then, the mountain has added 10 chairlifts, night skiing, a new base area and a ski-school facility. A boon to local powder skiers, it also happens to have some of the most accessible and best backcountry runs in the Northwest.

The plan around the bonfire the night of February 18 was to ski one of those backcountry runs. Tunnel Creek looks exactly like it sounds: a 42-degree, 2,500-vertical-foot slot that funnels into a tight drainage. There are alpine meadows and a few trees at the top. The farther you descend, the more the creek constricts and rolls over, until the drainage flattens out above a switchback on Highway 2.

Stifter and Carlsen met Jack the morning of the 19th and took a few runs in the 21 inches of fresh snow that had fallen. Around 11:00 a.m. they received a text from Rudolph that said to meet him outside the base lodge to ski Tunnel Creek. Wangen had shown them footage of the run the day before in his RV, and locals at the bar and around the bonfire had hailed it as one of the greatest powder slopes on the mountain.

The group met at an outdoor fire ring near the lodge, then took two chairlifts to the top of Cowboy Mountain. Around 11:30 a.m. a crew of 15 hiked from the top of the 7th Heaven chairlift through a gate marking the resort boundary, past a plastic sign warning skiers to proceed out of bounds at their own risk. It was a large crowd for a backcountry trip—ill-advised in most situations—but with so many seasoned locals like Jack, Rudolph and Brenan in the mix, most of the crew felt relatively confident.

That morning, Stifter, along with a few others, had read the Northwest Weather and Avalanche Center (NWAC) forecast. The report rated the avalanche danger as "considerable"—3 out of 5 on the avalanche danger scale—for that morning, meaning human-triggered slides were likely on certain aspects. Of particular concern was a layer of surface hoar frost—elongated crystals that grow on clear, cold nights and can collapse under the weight of new snow and cause avalanches—recently observed in the Stevens Pass area. Buried under two to three feet of new snow, the risk that the layer could fail had grown significantly.

But Stifter and others deferred to those who knew the slope best. The group had collectively skied Tunnel Creek hundreds of times and made the short hike from the gate to the summit of Cowboy quickly. Rob Castillo, an old ski buddy of Jack's who drove up from West Seattle with his wife and two children, had joined the expedition. He'd texted Brenan, who was having lunch in the RV with his daughters, and Brenan met them at the lift. Locals Wenzel Peikert and Wangen, along with Saugstad, Michelson, Abrams and Hammond—and three others who split off from the group at the summit—hiked the ridge as well.

Everyone partnered at the top and Castillo and Brenan agreed to keep an eye on each other. Castillo had worked for Brenan as a carpenter when he first moved to Leavenworth and they'd grown from skiers into family men together. They both had wives, children and full-time jobs. They'd survived a youth of skiing and partying, and, more impressively, managed to maintain much of it into their 40s.

Rudolph pushed off the ridge first and skied the upper section of Tunnel Creek, sinking into bottomless powder on every turn, a contrail of crystals shadowing him down the hill. The group whooped and he pulled into a stand of trees to wait. Saugstad, following backcountry protocol, waited until he stopped before heading down. She then floated through the snow with long, wide turns just to the right of Rudolph's tracks before pulling in beside him.

Castillo and Brenan were next in the lineup and looked at one another to decide who would go first. Obligations had kept Castillo from getting to Stevens as much as usual that winter, and Brenan knew his friend was itching to go. He gave him a nod and Castillo flashed him a grin. Castillo skied straight for 100 feet to gather speed, then turned into a large opening and arced graceful turns down the steep upper meadow. Brenan watched as he approached a cluster of trees in the middle of the slope. Castillo carved around them, angling right, then left. Brenan caught one last glimpse of Castillo's green helmet, then watched his friend disappear into a cloud of white.

Chapter Two

A Brief History

Announced by all the trumpets of the sky,

Arrives the snow, and, driving o'er the fields,

Seems nowhere to alight: the whited air

Hides hills and woods, the river, and the heaven,

And veils the farmhouse at the garden's end.

The sled and traveler stopped, the courier's feet

Delayed, all friends shut out, the housemates sit

Around the radiant fireplace, enclosed

In a tumultuous privacy of storm.

—*Ralph Waldo Emerson*

Every winter, an average of 105 winter storms strafe the contiguous United States. They hail from all points of the compass and blanket the earth with fluffy white snow. Poets write of the beauty and grace by which the flakes descend and quiet a scene. Meteorologists pull their hair out speculating where and when each storm will dump the most snow. Skiers watch the flakes and wax their boards, hoping it will never stop.

Snowstorms differ from other gales that traverse North America in that snow is exotic: the beauty and fragility of the crystals, the way they change a landscape for weeks or months at a time. Snow itself is classified as a mineral, because it is composed inorganically with an ordered atomic arrangement. Snowflakes form when water vapor freezes onto a dust particle in a cloud. From there, nature's simplest hydrogen-bonded crystal takes shape as a prism with six sides, a top and a bottom. Because ice grows faster at the edges of the prism, a depression forms in each face and six branches grow from the corners. As the flake falls to the ground, more water vapor freezes to the surface of the crystal and it grows more.

Most of the snow on Earth exists in the Northern Hemisphere, where coverage maxes out around 17.5 million square miles every winter. In the summer that number shrinks to around 730,000 square miles, mostly on the Greenland Ice Sheet and mountain glaciers. The scientific term for terrain where water exists in its solid form is cryosphere, derived from the Greek word *kryos*, meaning frost.

Blizzards have circled the Earth for millions of years. A snowstorm changed the course of history in 329 BC, when, after chasing Bessus across the Oxus and capturing the Persian crown, Alexander the Great lost 2,000 soldiers "frozen in place" in a snowstorm, eventually forcing him to return to Rome. In 1812, the "epiphany frosts" and snowfall of the Russian winter forced Napoleon and his Grand Army of 600,000 to retreat from a conquered Moscow. By the time they arrived in France, the living numbered 100,000. Closer to home, the Great Snow of 1717 hit New England in late February, leaving 25-foot snowdrifts, trapping residents of the young British colonies in their homes and giving credence to claims by settlers in the South that the Northeast was uninhabitable.

Ancient civilizations learned fairly quickly how to navigate through snow. The oldest skis on record date to 6300–5000 BC, excavated by Grigoriy Burov in the Vychegda Basin of Russia, 750 miles northwest of Moscow. The skis were preserved in a peat bog near Lake Sindor on the site of an ancient Mesolithic civilization. There was a carved moose head on the bottom of the ski, which Burov suggested could have been used for traction to go uphill—and as a symbol representing speed going downhill.[1]

Most prehistoric skis were used to hunt or forage. The 200 carved wooden boards that have been unearthed average 160 centimeters long and 15 centimeters wide. Hunters typically used a long staff when skiing, with a knife or spearhead on one end and a spoon-like tool on the other. One of the most remarkable characteristics of early skis, John B. Allen writes in his book, *The Culture and Sport of Skiing*, is how widespread their use was across the civilized world:

Skis discovered in other parts of the world defy the neatness of [the Scandinavian] systems. The Caribou Eskimos, in northern Canada, for example, used a narrow snowshoe-like board. Drawings of Siberian Samoyed and Ostyak from the seventeenth to the nineteenth centuries show semi-snowshoe, semi-ski footgear. If we look at the center of the ski on which the foot rests, we recognize similarities in geographically separate parts of the world. Not a few skis have two small pieces of wood attached on either side to help hold the foot in place. Their widespread distribution is as impressive as the longevity of their use. Such skis have been found north of Bergen, Norway, as they have been in Latvia (at Vecpicbalga) as well as in Bloke, Slovenia (seventeenth century-type) and in California (nineteenth century). The Norwegian Furnes ski is quite different, having a gouged out area in which the boot is placed, leaving the sides high. The same type of ski has been found as far away as Korea, where it may have been used in the marshes. Only one find has retained its binding, the Mänttä ski from Finland, dated to 500 AD. Part of a heel strap was still attached that had been made from badger skin. The pelt of the animal had also supplied an underlining to the ski. A similar binding was still in use in the 1890s in Norway.

There are mentions of skiing in early Chinese, Roman and Scandinavian writings. Rock carvings like the 4000 BC "Rødøy Hunter," discovered in 1929 in Norway, depict camouflaged hunters on long boards holding a single pole. The etchings and early descriptions suggest that a certain mysticism surrounded the sport—referencing hunters, warriors, kings and even gods cascading down a mountainside, staff in hand, ready to inflict a lethal blow on enemies or prey.

The appearance of the Norse gods Ullr (god of skiers) and Skade (goddess of skiers) in the thirteenth century Icelandic Eddas—two books of Norse mythology from the Viking era—added to the spirituality surrounding the discipline. The AD 1205 tale of two Birkebeiner skiing soldiers saving Swedish King Håkon III Sverresson's only son, and thus the kingdom—the prince tucked behind a shield, animal-hide boots strapped into Nordic fir skis—cemented skiing in the annals of history, as did this description in *The King's Mirror*, a Norwegian educational text published in AD 1250:

> It will seem even more miraculous when I tell them about men who know how to use pieces of wood or boards in the way that a man, who is no faster on foot than what people normally are as long as he has only shoes on his feet, becomes faster than a bird. As soon as he ties his boards, eight to nine yards long, he becomes faster than a bird or the fastest of Afghan dogs, and he can overtake a reindeer which runs doubly as fast as a deer. There are a great many people who can run on skis, so that they can keep up with reindeers, spearing nine or more of them. These things will sound incredible and strange in all those countries where people are ignorant about this art and the fact that just a board can give people such speed in the mountains. Nothing earthbound can measure up in speed to the man who has the boards on his feet, but as soon as he removes them, he is no faster than the others....Now we know for certain that during the winter, when we have snow, we have the opportunity to see many men who know the art of skiing.

It took a potato farmer in the Telemark region of Norway to evolve the art of skiing into a sport. Sondre Norheim and a few friends began the movement around 1860 after inventing a heel strap fashioned from birch root tendrils and, later, by shaping skis more like an hourglass from tip to tail. More importantly, where skis had been used to travel in straight lines in the past, Norheim and his cohorts developed a method to control speed and direction by turning. The "Telemark" and "Christiania" turns, which involved angling the base of the ski to turn, made skiing easier and, eventually, more accessible to the masses.

For the next two decades, Norheim and Norway's best skiers put on demonstrations in Christiania—present-day Oslo. Their fluid style and high-flying jumps made news across Europe. The Industrial Revolution had left the continent with a vastly expanded leisure class, many of whom had been vacationing in the Alps for years. The *beau monde* took a keen interest in the new sport and within 20 years Norway was exporting skis, and skiers, to Europe and North America—initiating a ski mania that would sweep across both continents.

Europe is generally considered the cradle of skiing, but the sport progressed just as quickly—and in some cases much faster—across the Atlantic. Most of America's early skiers were Norwegian immigrants, like Jon Torsteinson-Rue—aka "Snowshoe Thompson"—from Norway's Telemark region, who is credited with kicking off America's first skiing craze. In the 1850s, Thompson covered the eight-day winter mail run between Genoa, Nevada, and Placerville, California, in three and a half days. The feat made headlines in regional media and skiing became one of the primary means of winter transportation in high mountain towns in the Sierra Nevada.

It wasn't long before roughneck prospectors of the California Gold Rush found a way to challenge one another on skis, and make some money off of it. While wealthy patrons and their instructors held "ski tournaments" in the Alps and on the East Coast of America, Sierra racers at Onion Valley and La Porte, California, honed 12-foot "long boards" with custom sidecuts and carved bases to compete in the world's first downhill ski races—with purses equal to $2,000 today. The key to winning was custom ski wax called "dope"—a potion applied to the bottom of the skis that contained ingredients like buttermilk, furniture polish, whale oil and floor wax. Gamblers bet on the ski and dope designers as much as the skiers, the latter hitting speeds of up to 80 miles an hour on the straight, quarter-mile courses.[2]

The raucous Sierra ski scene dried up with the gold, and for the next 30 years American skiing kept pace with Europe—establishing clubs and, later, ski trains that chugged into the Appalachians, Rockies, Sierra and Cascades. By the mid-1930s there were 200 ski resorts and 150,000 skiers in the U.S. In 1936, Sun Valley, Idaho, installed the first chairlift in the world and the first issue of *Ski* magazine was published in Seattle. In 1941, though, World War II effectively ended ski development for the rest of the decade.

After the war, many of the troops from the 10th Mountain Division, who trained on skis in Colorado and fought in the mountains of Italy, returned to the States resolved to resurrect the American ski industry. More than 60 troops, like Vail founder Sgt. Pete Seibert, established resorts, and hundreds more taught skiing, founded ski magazines, designed skis, coached and opened ski shops. Ski areas proliferated in the East first, but when commercial flights made traveling west easier in the 1950s, resorts like Alta, Sun Valley and Aspen became the new hotbed of American skiing—and the sport evolved yet again.[3]

The peaks are taller and the plains wider out West. The sky is bigger and the sense of autonomy—of old-fashioned pioneering—is pervasive. Most ski towns in the Rockies still had mining operations in the 1950s and skiers mingled with miners, ranchers and locals descended from the country's first homesteaders. The westward migration was similar to the rustication movement of the Gilded Age in that the newcomers wanted to get their hands dirty and live close to the earth. The first seeds of ski bumming appeared then as college graduates roughed it in the hills for a season or two, then settled down to live on the land and wait for snow.

"This is the native home of hope," Wallace Stegner wrote of the American West. The cold, dry bite of morning air, the slow meter of Western speech, the way westerners talk about what's going on two valleys away—it is all so raw and real compared to the crowded coasts of the U.S. Land is fenced off in squares and many county roads are unpaved. In the summer, cottonwood and aspen grow in long green columns along the creeks, then turn gold in the fall. It can snow any month of the year in the high country, and locals wear jackets year-round. Pickup trucks case runway-wide boulevards downtown, past storefront façades and Civil War–era brick buildings. The stores and restaurants don't stay open late, but you can get breakfast just about anywhere at four-thirty in the morning.

The first ski-bum movement was an important time in American skiing, when the sport transformed from a weekend hobby into a lifestyle. As novelist James Salter, who moved to Aspen in the 1960s, wrote in an essay called "The Skiing Life" for *Outside* magazine, moving to a ski town meant *living* to ski, dropping out of the world you knew and immersing yourself in the one around you:

> When we lived in the East you drove for hours to ski and often waited in long lines. Skiing was a kind of pilgrimage. In Aspen it was different, it surrounded you, winter and skiing. There were the still-hot days of early October with the first white dusting of distant peaks, the nights growing colder, autumn ending, the blizzards and epic days, breakfast in town with exhaust drifting up in the cold from cars with glazed windows. The world was far away, in fact this was the world. To the south and west the clouds would turn dark blue, and a certain smell, like the smell of rain, lay in the air. Tremendous storms coming, the roof piled high with snow.

Powder skiing, and the subsequent freestyle revolution, exploded in the U.S. in the second half of the 20th century. Ski bums in Volkswagen buses took over Sun Valley, Aspen, Sugarloaf and Waterville Valley in the '60s, chasing powder on 210 centimeter Rossignol Stratos and plastic Koflach boots. Bobbie Burns, Dick Barrymore, Warren Miller, Wayne Wong, the K2 Performers and the "hotdogging" phenomenon got their start during this era—along with some of the first wet T-shirt contests in the world, conceived in Sun Valley's "Boiler Room" by Barrymore and Burns.

By the mid-'70s Dick Bass had opened Snowbird, Jackson Hole's iconic red tram was spinning and hippies in Telluride were driving mining families out of town—and installing their social agenda in local businesses and government. (Word has it the entire town tripped on acid for a day.) The early '80s saw skiers in Squaw Valley, Whistler and Taos smoking dope, burning skis for Ullr and chasing powder down any hill they could find their way to the top of. Soon thereafter—following the rise of the backcountry, "extreme skiing" and heli-ski phenomena—it became clear that powder skiing was America's first homegrown alpine sport.

Strangely, skiing's great arc started to flatten around that time. Rampant real estate development and skyrocketing lift ticket prices pushed locals out of town and off the hill, and seasonal owners transformed many mountain hamlets into ghost towns. Rising insurance and energy costs shuttered hundreds of ma-and-pa resorts, cutting off the sport to thousands of young skiers. The greatest innovation during that time was snowboarding, which bit into ski sales substantially and painted skiers as stodgy and passé. By the mid-'80s, profits were down in many regions and skier numbers were growing at a compounded annual rate of less than one percent. Baby boomers had grown older and distractions like TV, video games and a new crop of "life sports" had emerged. Then, in 1986, two designers working for Olin brought a ski to the Ski Industries America show in Las Vegas that changed the sport forever.

In 1984, an executive at Olin had asked Frank Meatto and Ed Pilpel to make a beginner ski so he could learn the sport. The "Albert" was constructed with more than four times the sidecut (hourglass shape) than traditional skis, meaning a skier could simply roll it on its side and make a turn, instead of flexing it—something only expert skiers typically could do. Though the prototype was too radical for retailers and didn't sell well, it helped spark 30 years of innovation and arguably one of the most dynamic sea changes in sporting history.[4]

From then on, each improvement seemed to spawn another. Soon after the Albert, Elan and K2 came out with more-advanced "shaped" skis—and Rupert Huber sawed a snowboard in half to make the world's first modern fat skis for Atomic. Canadian National Team mogul skier turned freeskier Mike Douglas followed, convincing Salomon to make the first high-performance twin-tip skis so he could land backwards in a halfpipe like snowboarders did. Three years later Volant released the first reverse-camber ski—invented by Shane McConkey after skiing with water skis on snow—initiating the "rocker" revolution. From there, designers perfected independent tip and tail camber and "progressive sidecut" (asymmetric hourglass shape), ultimately making powder skis so effortless to control, 70-year-olds could return to the slopes and ski like they were 50.

The effect that these innovations had on the upper echelons of the sport is hard to put into words. Imagine basketball players suddenly being able to leap from half court and slam-dunk a ball, or hockey players bending a slap shot 90 degrees. Where ski movies and magazine covers had depicted ski stars like Glen Plake and Kent Kreitler leaping off 40-foot cliffs in the 1990s, Jamie Pierre set a new world record in 2006 at 255 feet. (Swiss skier Fred Syversen broke it two years later with 355 feet.)

Wider dimensions and reverse camber allowed skiers to plane over, rather than through, the snow. Mountains from Colorado to Valdez, Alaska, that were unskiable in the past due to avalanche danger were suddenly tracked up by giant high-speed turns—with skiers literally outrunning avalanches on fat skis. Super-lightweight gear allowed a growing number of backcountry skiers to penetrate deeper into the mountains, and skiers in Europe started using small parachutes to "speed ride" down slopes—essentially parachuting with skis a few feet above the snow. Then McConkey and J.T. Holmes pioneered ski-B.A.S.E. jumping, leaping off 2,000-foot cliffs and opening a parachute.

The higher skiers soared and the faster they went, the smaller the margin of error grew. It was only a matter of time before the inevitable happened. Skiers started dying. The first fatalities were in the backcountry, with a lethal five-year spate from 2001 to 2006 that took down eminent ski mountaineers Hans Saari, Alex Lowe, Carl Skoog and Doug Coombs, among others. The skiing world reeled when McConkey fell to his death attempting a ski-B.A.S.E. jump in Italy in 2009. The winter of 2010–2011 proved more tragic when six professional skiers died in the mountains. After nine more were killed in the 2011–2012 season, including Pierre and superstar Sarah Burke, the national media took note.

Powder ran a black cover with the question "Why Do the Best Skiers Keep Dying?" and an 18-page feature by managing editor Matt Hansen. NBC's "Rock Center" with Brian Williams broadcast a nine-minute exposé titled "The Death Zone," which questioned why expert skiers put themselves at such seemingly unnecessary risk. Squaw Valley ski-movie veteran and psychiatrist Dr. Robb Gaffney appeared in the segment and said that he had lost five friends in three years, including McConkey. He speculated that there would be more deaths in the future if something didn't change and founded the website Sportgevity.com to address risk-taking in the professional sports community. The organization's mission statement: "Dedicated to making our sports lifelong passions."

A second series of headlines, from a completely different angle, painted an even grimmer picture of the future of skiing. The 2011–2012 season had not only been one of the deadliest years in the sport—it had also been one of the warmest. Half of the nation's ski areas opened late and almost half closed early. What's more, 9 of the 10 warmest years on record had occurred since 2000—and several peer-reviewed scientific papers suggested that climate change would wipe out the snowpack in the Western United States by 25 to 100 percent by the year 2100.[5]

A few weeks after Hurricane Sandy elevated the global-warming conversation to the presidential level, the *Boston Globe* ran an article titled "Climate Change Threat Looms over Ski Industry." The piece suggested that half of the Northeast's 103 ski areas would have to close in the next 30 years because it simply would be too warm to expect or make snow. Subsequent reports predicted a similar fate for Sierra and Northwestern ski resorts by mid- to late century. A study from the University of Colorado speculated that if global warming continued on its current track, average winter temperatures in Aspen would climb 8.5 degrees Fahrenheit, and 10.5 degrees Fahrenheit in Park City, by 2100, essentially spelling the end of skiing for all but a few inland, high-elevation resorts in the West. A report from the Global Snow Lab at Rutgers University followed, pointing out that spring snow cover in the Northern Hemisphere has already shrunk on average by one million square miles in the past 45 years.

The possibility of no snow in mid-latitude regions—including all of Europe and much of the Lower 48 by 2100—seemed absurd to the ski community. Yet, as climate science evolves and warming continues, just such a fate is becoming more probable. Which is to say that at the moment when humans have learned to master the sport they invented 8,000 years ago—and truly fly like the gods—it is entirely possible that it will no longer exist by the end of the century.

Chapter Three

The Skiing Life

In order to understand this ongoing process of learning from powder snow, it is necessary to realize that when one skis in deep powder snow, there is absolutely nothing there—no resistance whatsoever. There is no "thing" to push against in order to turn as one does in regular skiing.... Our culture has no words for this experience of "nothing" when skiing powder. In general the idea of nothingness or no-thing in our culture is frightening. However, in Chinese Taoist thought, it's called "the fullness of the void" out of which all things come.

–*Dolores LaChapelle*, Deep Powder Snow

Rob Castillo had driven Highway 2 dozens of times before packing the family SUV the afternoon of February 17 and heading to Stevens Pass. The 41-year-old moved to West Seattle after marrying his wife, Pamela, but before that he'd lived in a small cabin outside of Leavenworth. Castillo was a ski bum in the old sense of the word. He'd left everything he knew as an 18-year-old in Westchester, New York, in 1989 and disappeared into the mountains. He lived in powder meccas like Crested Butte, Colorado, and Alta, Utah, and road-tripped to others with a cadre of like-minded powder junkies he met along the way—sleeping in cars, working service jobs, driving through the night to chase storms across the West and logging more than 100 days a year on skis.

Castillo got hooked the way a lot of people who grew up skiing in the East do. His father had schussed around the Alps in the 1960s and took him to Hunter Mountain in upstate New York when he was young. After a few ski trips to icy slopes on the Byram Hills High

School bus, he saw his first ski magazine, contemplated the rimed peaks and waist-deep powder of the Rockies and thought to himself, "One day I'll be there."

Castillo didn't take up skiing seriously until he enrolled at the University of New Hampshire. Friends taught him how to keep his upper body still and follow the fall line on Loon Mountain's blue runs. He read about ski technique and practiced whenever he could get away from school, then landed a gig teaching skiing to kids. His junior year, he heard about an exchange program UNH had with Western State Colorado University in Gunnison, Colorado—30 miles from Crested Butte—and stayed up all night applying and gathering signatures from advisors.

Castillo spent the winter of 1992–1993 at Western State, but put in more time on Crested Butte's steep, rock-lined slopes than in the classroom—skiing five days a week, living in a shotgun shack near the A&W in Gunnison and riding his bike to school on the occasional days he attended. He took more than a few tumbles on the 12,162-foot mountain's demanding runs, especially when it snowed and the slopes disappeared beneath a thick blanket of Colorado powder. Powder skiing is a different sport compared to what most eastern skiers know. It requires subtle shifts of weight instead of powerful angling and turning. Similar to waterskiing, if a powder skier slows down, he sinks. So you have to commit to the fall line and head straight downhill to gather speed before your first turn—a terrifying prospect for anyone who grew up on the icy, boilerplate runs of the Northeast.

Powder skiing was the first kind of skiing—because in the beginning there were no trails, lifts or grooming machines to speak of. One of America's greatest contributions to the discipline came in the 1940s when Alta's first ski-school director, Dick Durrance, pioneered the modern powder turn. Living at the foot of a sheer 10,550-foot mountain that received more than 40 feet of snow every year, Durrance had little choice but to invent a technique to navigate the mountain's tight chutes. He devised the "Dipsy Doodle"—essentially stepping through a turn, one ski at a time. The method was improved by his successors and friends, including Alf Engen, Dolores LaChapelle, Jim and Elfrieda Shane, Junior Bounous and Jim McConkey (Shane's father). Bounous's subsequent Double Dipsy was groundbreaking not only in that it allowed more control in powder snow—it also was easier to learn and led many U.S. skiers away from rigid European tradition and into the great powder fields of the backcountry.

Skiing untracked snow ignited the American spirit of innovation and adventure—already running hot following World War II—and spread through the West quickly. Along with the freedom of skiing where and how you wanted, a new spirituality arose, an almost cult belief in the higher power of skiing powder that harkened back to medieval skiing kings and gods. LaChapelle was the most vocal of the early powder skiers and collected her essays and memories in a 1993 book called *Deep Powder Snow*, still considered by many to be the bible of the sport:

> My experiences with powder snow gave me the first glimmerings of the further possibilities of the mind. Because of a snowfall so heavy that I could not see the steep angle of the slope, I learned to ski powder snow quite suddenly, when I discovered that I was not turning the skis, but that the snow was—or rather the snow and gravity together were turning the skis. I then quit trying to control the skis and turned them over to these forces. Now, to begin a run all I need do is point the skis downhill. As they begin moving, I push down with my heels so that the tips can rise just enough for the snow to lift them. As I feel this lift, I respond as I come up by turning the tips ever so slightly out of the fall line to the right. Immediately I feel the snow turning them and then gravity takes over and finishes the turn. At a certain point in this process, I am totally airborne, but then, as I feel myself being pulled down, I cooperate with gravity and again push down on my heels and feel the snow lift the skis once again. This time I begin to move the skis to the left and once more the snow and gravity finish the turn. Once this rhythmic relationship to snow and gravity

is established on a steep slope, there is no longer an "I" and snow and the mountain, but a continuous flowing interaction. I know this flowing process has no boundaries. My actions form a continuum with the actions of the snow and gravity. I cannot tell exactly where my actions end and the snow takes over, or where or when gravity takes over.

Dolores and Ed LaChapelle were an instant legend when they moved to Alta in 1952. Ed, who was a geophysicist, took over the Western Hemisphere's first avalanche research center there, started by Montgomery Atwater in the 1940s. Dolores raised their newborn son, Randy, while pioneering the steep trees and gullies of Alta. She skied almost every day, often with Randy on her back. In 1956, she made the first descent of Alta's renowned Baldy Chute with Jim Shane.

With the introduction of new techniques and equipment—like the short, fat, powder-friendly Miller Softs in 1952—powder skiing spread further into the mainstream. Dick Barrymore screened films of skiers gliding through "cold smoke" around the country, narrating the shows live. After living in a teardrop trailer in the Sun Valley parking lot for years, Warren Miller released *Deep and Light* in 1949 and continued to make a ski movie every year for the next half century.

After two decades in Alta, the LaChapelles landed in Silverton, Colorado. They amicably parted ways soon thereafter, and Dolores stayed in Silverton—walking a route through town every day, delivering books to friends and leading t'ai chi classes. I'd read her book many times as a young skier and writer and tracked her down one day in 2006 while I was on an assignment in Silverton.

I remember her house was small and bright. Inside was a cross section of a tree that had been split by lightning and grown back together. The walls, ceilings and floor were planked with pine and there was a large cast-iron woodstove in the living room. The place smelled like tea, and, as it turned out, Dolores was brewing a pot in the kitchen. She stood slightly hunched over, surveyed me up and down and without saying a word led me to a sunny alcove and sat down. She wasn't happy that I was there, but she wasn't unhappy either. It seemed as if she was waiting to see if I was going to waste her time. The windows in the alcove looked out onto the giant peaks surrounding Silverton. There was a bench in the yard that she had situated to look out on something she called an "intentional landscape."

She talked about skiing for a while and lamented the modern era of high-speed lifts and fancy equipment. She'd lived in the days when a lift ticket cost 25 cents and friends made skis for each other in their woodshops. Powder was unlimited; you just had to get to it and know how to ski it. The giant corporation that had taken over skiing since then was just too much, she said.

Dolores died less than a year after our conversation. Friends, family and admirers attended her memorial to express their gratitude and condolences. Ed came as well. After the memorial, he went skiing at the Monarch Ski Area in Colorado with his partner, Meg Hunt, and friends. He was skiing knee-deep powder when he had a heart attack and died. He and Dolores were both 80 years old.

Castillo's first memories of powder were of cartwheeling through it as he tried to get the hang of it. By spring, though, he could hold his own on the mountain's most difficult runs. He was naturally athletic—5 foot 11 with a solid build, chestnut brown hair and a joker's smile. He was lucky to come of age as a skier during a pivotal time in the sport, when equipment and technique were leaping forward after years of stasis. He remembers seeing 17-year-old Seth Morrison—harbinger of where skiing would go—ski at Mach speed beside the High Lift Poma, then Jim Jack flash past, while he was filming *Soul Sessions and Epic Impressions* with two young cinematographers who would found the seminal ski-film production company Matchstick Productions.

After he graduated from UNH, Castillo moved out West—first to Crested Butte, then Aspen, where a friend had rented a house on the ski hill. The day Castillo moved in, he heard about a 60-inch snowstorm in Alta and jumped into his Subaru station wagon and drove straight to Little Cottonwood Canyon. He pulled into the Goldminer's Daughter Lodge later that night to stay with another friend from college. By 11:00 a.m. the next morning he had secured a job at the lodge, a free season pass and a room for the winter. He didn't return to Aspen to collect his things for two months.

The Goldminer's Daughter has been an institution in Alta and the ski-bum world since LaChapelle's friends, Jim and Elfrieda Shane, built it in 1961. Compensation for employees includes a season pass, a shared double room in the hotel and three meals a day. Payment starts at $100 a week, but with food, shelter and 2,000 vertical feet of powder outside your door, there's little need for money.

Castillo formed ranks with skiers on his hallway and, after prepping food at night for the Top of the Lodge Restaurant, he continued his education in the intricacies of powder skiing. He befriended Jim Jack, who had moved there from Crested Butte and was working as a maître d' at the restaurant. Jocular and overbrimming with energy, "the man with three first names" had already been dubbed "The Mayor of Alta," simply because everyone knew him. (A phenomenon that followed Jack wherever he went.)

The pair spent most of their paychecks on Jim Beam bourbon at the Alta Lodge liquor store and watched *Soul Sessions* dozens of times in their rooms. Staff quarters were a holdover from the '70s, with quilted patchwork bedspreads, nightstands, TVs, bureaus and a closet for skis and clothes. Castillo's window faced the Transfer tow rope, and he could peek outside and gauge how much snow had fallen the night before—which was record-breaking his first winter at 745 inches. It was a ski-bum's paradise in every way, where employees drank whiskey and jawed about skiing late into the night, then woke at dawn to catch the first chairlift and push their limits on the hill.

Castillo's first backcountry run was with Jack and a few others in Wolverine Cirque, a crescent-moon-shaped bowl one ridge north of Alta. His boss let him borrow an avalanche beacon with the caveat, "Make sure you turn it on so I get it back either way." Castillo had long been wary of avalanches—at first from ignorance of what triggered them, then later from stories about how they took out even the most experienced alpinists. Alta itself, set at the head of Little Cottonwood Canyon, was built in a slide path and had a long history of battling the "white dragon"—starting with Montgomery Atwater and Ed LaChapelle.

Castillo returned the beacon unharmed and went on to take avalanche-safety courses and overnight backcountry trips and eventually ski the granddaddy of the Wasatch Mountains, 11,132-foot Mount Superior. When Dave McReynolds and a group of aspiring pro skiers from California moved to the Goldminer's Daughter the following year, Castillo followed them the entire season.

There are moonlighters and lifers in the ski-bum world. The short-hitters ramble out West for a while, ski hard, party harder, meet a girl or get a job and slowly wander away from the mountains. Lifers drift a bit too, but in smaller circles, inevitably returning to the high country every winter to figure out how to score a pass and build a "powder clause" into their employment contract. If they stick with it long enough, lifers ascend into a realm of skiing that only a small coterie of skiers in America ever knows. They're not pros, they're not necessarily in ski movies or magazines, but they are masters of the sport. The act of skiing itself becomes secondary, the muscle movements so ingrained that their minds wander mid-run to route choice, snow consistency, avalanche hazard and what they want to make for dinner.

Six years after he moved to Alta, Castillo entered that elite circle of skiers and started traveling to ski competitions with McReynolds and Jack. Shane McConkey was in the process of founding the International Free Skiing Association (IFSA) to consolidate a movement that until then didn't have an official name. The skiing was defined by big lines and big air and, recently, big skis. A key element of the movement was a series of Freeskiing World Tour (FWT) competitions, run by Mountain Sports International, set on high-alpine peaks where professional and amateur freeskiers showed off their skills. Castillo, Jack and McReynolds traveled to contests in Crested Butte, Snowbird, Kirkwood and Whistler for four years. They usually placed top 20, though Jack and McReynolds broke the top 10. It was a laudable result, considering the competition was threading rocky faces at 60 miles an hour and throwing backflips off 50-foot cliffs.

Castillo took his first trip to Valdez, Alaska—the latest proving ground of the freeskiing movement—in 1996. Doug Coombs had been exploring the Chugach Mountains near Valdez for years, opening it to film and magazine crews first, then expert heli-ski clients from all over the world. Castillo and McReynolds ended up at Alaska Backcountry Adventures down the highway from Coombs, where they bought 500 dollars' worth of poker chips that ABA used as tokens for rides. (A nod to the addictive nature of heli-skiing in Alaska.)

Castillo's friend and fellow wine steward from Alta, Dan Caruso, was their guide the first day. The helicopter dropped them off on a near-vertical snowcapped peak 5,000 feet above Prince William Sound. The group descended to the mouth of a 3,000-foot couloir stacked with powder. Halfway down the chute, Caruso told Castillo and McReynolds to ski a chute that branched off to the right. When Castillo skied into it, a 40-foot-wide avalanche broke off above him.

He tried to set an edge and hold on, but giant blocks of snow started hitting him in the back. As the debris rushed around and beneath him, he pointed his skis straight downhill to gain enough speed to turn out of the slide path. He'd just bought his first pair of fat skis and happened to be riding them that day. It was a good choice, as they rose to the top of the mess quickly, allowing him to angle left to a rocky knob. From there, he watched the avalanche that would have buried him surge past.

McReynolds was standing above the fracture line when it broke and by the time the avalanche exploded into a snow cloud 2,000 feet below, he had his avalanche transceiver set to search. The pair took a moment, then skied through the debris to the rest of the group. For the remainder of the trip, the thought that a slope could snap at any time never left Castillo's mind.

A lot happened between that day in Valdez and February 19, when Castillo headed to Stevens Pass to meet Jim Jack for a run. Castillo had met the woman he would marry and moved from Alta to Leavenworth to be closer to her. He skied Stevens and the skyscraping Cascadian peaks surrounding it with Jack as often as possible and took a job as a carpenter with Jack's friend, Johnny Brenan. When Castillo put an offer on a small cabin he wanted to buy, Jack convinced the owner of a local pub to say that Castillo was a full-time employee, so he could get a loan. The day Castillo closed the deal, the two friends cracked a beer at the cabin and made a pact to ski every peak they could see from the porch.

The pact had long been met when Castillo got married and moved to West Seattle. Jack and McReynolds stood by his side at the wedding. It was a fairytale story for a ski bum, given the fact that his wife, Pamela, liked to ski and they drove the Stevens Pass Highway on the weekends to stay at the cabin. February 19 wasn't any different. The kids were still asleep when Castillo woke and he spent a few minutes looking at Big Jack Mountain, which he and Jack had notched the first descent on. That winter had been strange in a few ways: lots of snow, then lots of rain. Even stranger, Jack and Castillo hadn't skied a run together all year.

They'd been in touch the day before, though, and planned to meet on the hill at 11:00 a.m. Jack was already skiing when Castillo arrived with his family. After putting his son in ski school and handing off their daughter to a friend, he and Pamela took a lap together. At the bottom Jack texted that they were getting ready to ski Tunnel Creek. Castillo kissed Pamela goodbye, grabbed a coffee and met the group. An hour later, at the top of Cowboy Mountain, he pushed off into Tunnel Creek for his first powder run with Jack of the year.

Castillo made a few turns in the knee-deep snow, crystals sticking to his stubble and swirling over his shoulders. He saw Rudolph and Saugstad in the trees below and pulled in beneath them. Brenan came next and the group cheered as he vanished under a plume of powder, then emerged and made another turn. While they waited, Castillo noticed that Tim Wangen and Wenzel Peikert had skied to a ridgeline nearby and wondered if it would be safer to join them on high ground—beyond the reach of a potential avalanche. He asked the others if they should move, and everyone agreed.

The group prepped their gear as the next skier dropped into the meadow high above. Castillo pulled out his Avalung—a device that helps you breathe if you're buried in a slide—as a precaution. He was fiddling with his gloves when he first heard the sound. He knew what it was before he saw it. He'd heard it before. By the time he looked up, the 25-foot-tall wall of snow rushing down the hill was 100 feet away.

He didn't try to grab his Avalung's mouthpiece. He knew there wasn't time. The chute dropped practically straight down from where they were standing, tightening to a 60-foot-wide elevator shaft lined with trees and cliffs. Instead, he turned his skis sideways across two trees directly below him, each trunk 10 inches in diameter. Then he wrapped his arms around both and stuck his head between them to keep from getting knocked unconscious by the impact.

He didn't know what the other skiers were doing. He didn't know if Brenan and Rudolph had tried to ski away. He didn't even know who set the slide off or how many people were caught in it. All he knew was that he had a wife and two children waiting for him at the base lodge. And the only way he was going to see them again was to hang on.

Chapter Four
The Great Melt

Now there is one outstanding important fact regarding Spaceship Earth, and that is that no instruction book came with it.

—*Buckminster Fuller*

B oulder Valley unfurls from the eastern fringe of the Rocky Mountains in a checkerboard carpet, wrapping around the bricked streets of the city set in its center. At the edge of town, beyond a patchwork of suburbs built on ranchland once cleared by homesteaders, the valley meets the Great Plains, which continue uninterrupted 500 miles east to the Mississippi River. Behind the Boulder skyline, just before the mountains' sudden rise, the auburn sedimentary stone faces of the Flatirons stand as sentinels of the Front Range—the 300-mile eastern edge of the greatest mountain range in the Western Hemisphere.

Colorado is Mountain Country, the Rocky Mountain State and the Switzerland of America. There are more 14,000-foot peaks within its borders than in any other state in the Union, and millions of skiers congregate there every winter. The serrated ridgelines running behind the Flatirons wend up to the Continental Divide and the first summits of the Rockies. Every fall, the first snow of the year dusts them white, and by January they are rimed and coated in a thick white blanket. There are still a few squares of pasture around the edges of the city, delineated by buck-and-rail fences and browning grass. Close to the highway, rows of storage facilities and municipal bike paths hemming in the historic Gunbarrel and Boulder Valley ranches attest to the great population that now calls Boulder home.

Storms arrive in the valley in long, wispy lines with feathered ridges. The maelstroms rage over the plains, the suburbs of Denver, fast-food joints along Highway 36 and, eventually, the tan buildings of the University of Colorado in downtown Boulder. A few blocks away, in a three-story brick building off 30th Street, scientists who've spent most of their lives observing such fronts pore over computer monitors, trying to decipher what weather will come next week—or, as is the case these days, in the next century.

The National Snow and Ice Data Center (NSIDC) is bordered by a row of pine trees and a skinny parking lot for visitors. Inside, scientists wearing fleece vests and running shoes collect data from two dozen polar-orbiting and low-inclination satellites circling the Earth. NSIDC began as a library in the United States Geological Survey office in Tacoma, Washington. It was called the World Data Center for Glaciology then and recorded data, mostly on sea ice for the Navy, on cold regions of the planet. After moving to Boulder, it became what amounted to a server farm to store the billions of bytes of information that NASA satellites send home every year.

NASA has been studying the Earth since the agency was created in 1958. It sent its first Earth-observing satellites into orbit shortly there-after, but didn't start recording reliable satellite observations of snow and ice until the late 1970s. After mumblings in Congress that govern-ment-funded scientists knew more about the surface of Mars than they did about their own planet, NASA initiated its "Mission to Planet Earth" program in 1991—with a proposal to launch $30 billion of satellites into orbit and point them toward Earth instead of space.[6]

The plan was ambitious, including a half dozen 15-ton satellites loaded with sensors that measure things like the Earth's land composition, reflective energy, vegetation, snow, ice, aerosols and carbon monoxide.

Some members of Congress said it promoted a global-warming agenda and quashed the initiative. NASA had recently released the first reports of a potential hole in the ozone layer, and conservatives viewed any discussion of the atmosphere or emissions as a threat to commerce and the economy at large. The conjecture that human behavior was affecting something on a planetary scale was still considered preposterous and anti-capitalist and had no place in government.

What climatologists knew at the time, and had known for ages, was that a layer of "greenhouse gases" like water vapor kept the planet about 50 degrees Fahrenheit warmer than it would be without them. Increased levels of greenhouse gases created by humans since the beginning of the Industrial Revolution in 1750—including carbon dioxide, methane and nitrous oxide—have warmed the planet further. The cause is largely burning fossil fuels in power plants, vehicles, buildings and industries. Fewer trees on the planet to absorb carbon dioxide exacerbates the problem, as do things like commercial livestock operations and landfills that emit large amounts of methane—which is more than 20 times more potent a greenhouse gas than carbon dioxide.

The planet has gone through warming and cooling cycles before, mostly due to solar activity, volcanic eruptions and wobbles in the Earth's orbit. Around 55 million years ago the global temperature rose 10.4 degrees Fahrenheit, and more than 30 degrees Fahrenheit at the poles. The warming trend was accompanied by a release of more than 2,500 gigatons of carbon into the ocean and atmosphere, possibly caused by volcanic activity beneath the ocean floor.[7] Rapid warming is not unheard of either. As recently as the last Ice Age, several regions saw temperatures rise up to 18 degrees Fahrenheit in just a few decades. That period lasted a few hundred years and was most likely the result of a disturbance in how ocean currents distribute heat.

Carbon data drawn from air bubbles trapped in Antarctic ice hundreds of thousands of years ago—in addition to fossil coral, stalagmite and fossil tree-ring evidence millions of years old—shows that significant changes in atmospheric carbon dioxide levels correlate with warming and cooling trends. When carbon dioxide levels are high, the Earth is warm; when they're low, it's cooler. The gas is a kind of regulator for the world's climate: adding a significant amount of it into the atmosphere has the same effect as cranking up the thermostat in your house. With 500 billion tons of human-created carbon released into the air over the last two and a half centuries—a quarter of the 55-million-year warming-event level—and that number projected to double in 40 years, scientists are saying the current warming trend could be like no other in history.[8]

Generally, the Earth has been cooling for the last 50 million years and for the last 2.6 million has fluctuated between Ice Ages and 10,000- to 30,000-year interglacial periods. We are in an interglacial period now, 11,500 years after the last Ice Age thawed. Modern civilization blossomed during this period of temperate, stable climatic conditions, presumably because it facilitates abundant food production. As humans spread around the globe, populations came to expect rain at certain times of the year and snow in others. Over the centuries, cultural and national identities, as well as industries like skiing and growing wine grapes, formed in various climate zones. These days, though, many of those regions are shifting, fast.

Average temperatures around the globe have already increased 1.4 degrees Fahrenheit since the 1800s. The last decade was the warmest on record, and the three decades prior were each hotter than the last, all setting new temperature records. With humans releasing 90 million tons of carbon into the atmosphere every day, carbon dioxide levels are on track to match those of the 55-million-year warming event, and it's probable that further natural greenhouse gas emissions from melting permafrost and the ocean will push temperatures even higher.[9] What scientists have been trying to figure out, beginning with the Mission to Planet Earth program, is when that might happen and how to slow or stop it.

Mission to Planet Earth was eventually stripped down and given the more business-friendly name Earth Science Enterprise (ESE). NASA launched the program's flagship satellite, Terra, on December 18, 1999, from California's Vandenberg Air Force Base. The ESE mission was the largest data-collecting project in non-military history, with early satellites filling 270,000 magnetic cassettes every year. ESE's goal was to gather information on the atmosphere, oceans, land, ice and snow, then deliver the data to researchers who could interpret the information.[10]

The initiative was a boon for Boulder-based NSIDC, charged with storing all of the new data, and soon researchers there began studying the science of the numbers they were archiving. Of particular interest was a dramatic loss of ice on the poles. The first large-scale reduction of sea ice was observed in the late 1990s. Images of polar bears stranded on floating icebergs and of calving glaciers caught the public's attention in a way climate-change literature never had. For years, "global warming" existed as an abstract concept to most, similar to killer meteorites and the possibility of the sun imploding in a few billion years. To see climate change in the 1990s, though, all you had to do was look north.

Sea ice in the Arctic and the massive ice sheets covering Greenland and Antarctica started melting at a rate never seen before, and every major media outlet called NSIDC to track it. The influx of attention to the once-sleepy facility was so intense, the center had to hire its first receptionist to field all the calls. "Before climate change was in the forefront," says NSIDC senior research scientist Dr. Richard Armstrong, "you'd go to an international glaciology meeting and there might be 50 people there. Now you go and there's 50 people in every one of 10 sessions every day. Because there's no more-obvious indicator of global warming than the reduction of sea ice and glaciers....It's a single polygon that grows and shrinks and has a trend over time. And it's easy for people to see it and go, 'Whoa, it's disappearing.' As opposed to a change in tree line—not so easy to grasp."

Armstrong has been with NSIDC for 30 years, served as its interim director and is currently working for the U.S. Agency for International Development in the Himalayas, determining glacial contributions to water supplies in 10 countries the mountains straddle. He is 69 years old with clear blue eyes and thinning blond hair. He has a Colorado look about him: wiry 5-foot-10 frame, sloped Robert Mitchum eyes and a bushy east-west mustache that turns north-south on either end. It's easy to imagine him shouldering a pair of skis with a rooster hat and goggles, probably because that is exactly what he does every winter day that he's not in the lab or on the road.

Armstrong was introduced to snow the way many snow scientists are: by learning to ski. He grew up in Casper, Wyoming, and took his first run at the local city-owned ski hill. After teaching skiing in Switzerland, he entered the University of Washington snow science program—where he was introduced to the North Cascades and a man who seems to exist at the center of all things snow: Ed LaChapelle.

Before snow started disappearing, the biggest problem was that there was too much of it. For thousands of years civilizations have been haunted by the vision of a wall of snow careening down a mountainside. In medieval times Europeans engraved book covers with images of evil spirits lurking in the high peaks, and most considered mountains and snow props of the devil.

If avalanches were long-feared in Europe, they were a complete mystery in America. LaChapelle was one of the first avalanche researchers in the States and was the first American to study at the storied Swiss Federal Commission for Snow and Avalanche Research in Davos. When LaChapelle got a contract at UW in 1968 to forecast avalanches on Red Mountain Pass near Silverton, Colorado, he brought along one of his prodigies, Armstrong, to help. "In the old days they would keep the pass open until a car got hit," Armstrong says. "Then they decided there's gotta be a better way. So we developed a forecast model so they could close the gates and try to do it that way."

Armstrong skied into the heart of the white dragon five days a week during his time in Silverton. He and his wife, Betty, lived near the Christ of the Mines Shrine, a 12-ton, 16-foot-tall homage on Anvil Mountain to the town's mining past. He skied between Red Mountain Pass and Silverton for work, checking study plots and taking a powder run when there was time. He learned everything he could from LaChapelle, then moved to Fort Collins to work for the U.S. Forest Service's mountain meteorology and forecast center. When the USFS cut the program in 1985, he continued his work at NSIDC.

Armstrong is tight-lipped when it comes to the future of snow. Like his mentor, he is a man of science, takes pride in being accurate and backing up claims with solid evidence. He has no interest in politics or "alarmists" and relies on numbers to explain things. He worked in relative obscurity until NSIDC landed in the spotlight in the 1990s—then again in 2007, when the most visible face in the world of climate change walked through the door.

Al Gore was preparing for a speech in Boulder that year when one of his aides mentioned that "the place that collects all the sea-ice data" was just down the road. Gore set up a meeting and the following day his signature cavalcade of Priuses rolled down 30th Street to NSIDC. Armstrong and a team of scientists met with him for hours around several tables in the basement. Soon after, Armstrong contributed to a report for the United Nations Environment Programme and, later, a paper commissioned by Gore himself.

The former vice president wanted a document that explained, in layman's terms, how much ice and snow was currently melting and what that meant for the planet. *Melting Snow and Ice: A Call for Action* was presented at the United Nations Climate Change Conference in Copenhagen in 2009. The 70-page report made it clear that the cryosphere was melting faster and more completely than anyone previously thought. Arctic sea ice was disappearing at many times the predicted rate, and an ice-free Arctic Ocean was deemed possible by mid-century. Surface melt and ice flow into the ocean had accelerated in Greenland to five times the forecasted rate, and melting land ice had become the dominant contributor to sea-level rise, the rate of which had doubled since 1993.[11]

Relative to the history of temperature and sea level, carbon content in the atmosphere was already approaching a dangerous level. The last time it was as high as it is now, during the Pliocene epoch three million years ago, the oceans rose 30 to 60 feet—flooding the North American coastline up to 90 miles inland. If Greenland and Antarctica were to completely melt out—including the eastern Antarctic ice shelf—it would raise sea levels by 220 feet.

The Northern Hemisphere has been warming faster than its southern counterpart since the 1980s, though South America, New Zealand, Australia and Antarctica have also seen record melting. In terms of snow, the report found that the mean monthly snow-cover extent in the Northern Hemisphere was decreasing at about 1.5 percent per decade. Monthly maximum snow-water equivalent—the amount of water in snow if it were to melt—was expected to decrease 60 to 80 percent throughout mid-latitude regions by 2100, with the largest declines projected for Europe, the west coast of North America, Scandinavia and the Pacific coast of Russia.

In the U.S., the rate of winter warming in the Lower 48 has tripled since 1970. The strongest warming is in the northern and western parts of the country. Coastal ranges, where winter temperatures hover close to the freezing level, are seeing the most significant change in snowfall. The Pacific Northwest could receive 40 to 70 percent less snow by 2050 on our current track. The snowpack in British Columbia has declined by half overall and the ski season in some regions is four to five weeks shorter than it was 50 years ago. Eastern Canada is even warmer, with the ski season in southern Quebec predicted to drop to less than two months. In Tahoe, spring now arrives two and a half weeks earlier at 6,000 feet, and computer models show the Northeast ski season shrinking to less than 100 days by 2039. Under other models, the mean snow depth for the Rocky Mountains is predicted to drop to zero by 2100.[12]

The problem is worse in the European Alps, where temperatures are rising three times faster than the global average. Since 1850, European glaciers have lost half of their volume—26 percent of that loss since the 1970s alone. In the French Alps, snowfall levels dropped 25 inches on average between 1960 and 2007. In the summer of 2012, iconic peaks like the Matterhorn and the Aiguille du Midi were snow- and ice-free for the first time in recorded history. With predictions of up to 5.4 degrees Fahrenheit of warming by 2050—and a 500-vertical-foot rise in the freezing level for every 1.8 degree Fahrenheit of warming—two-thirds of the 666 ski areas in Europe in the UNEP report Armstrong contributed to would have to close by mid-century.[13]

Climatologists are still struggling to understand the relationship between global circulations and climate change, and skeptics rightly point out that meteorologists have a hard enough time predicting the weather a week out, much less a century. But with 97 percent of climatologists in agreement that human-created greenhouse gases are warming the planet[14]—and an equal degree of assurance from the IPCC's 2013 report—it is probable that most skiers today will see change in their lifetimes.

Many find it laughable to call a lack of skiing a global crisis. In part, they are right. Skiing is a sport, a voluntary act practiced by those who can afford it. What's more, the industry's carbon footprint—including equipment manufacturing, resort operations and the travel it takes to get to the mountain—is sizeable. What has scientists, environmentalists and mountainfolk worried is not a lack of fresh tracks, though. It is a lack of snow itself—which is a vital component of the Earth's water cycle and climate system. As people living in the Western U.S. have already seen, declining snow depth is the first domino in a long line that can set off a downward spiral of environmental catastrophes.

Thinning spring snowpack and glaciers means less natural water storage and runoff in the warm months. Resulting dry conditions have already led to increased wildfires in the West, like the record blazes of 2013 that devastated Yosemite and much of Colorado, Idaho and New Mexico. River habitat, hydroelectric plants and thousands of species living downstream of the high peaks also are affected. An infestation of mountain pine beetles, brought on by warm, dry winters, has ravaged 23 million acres of forestland since 2000. Lack of snowmelt also has contributed to the extended drought gripping almost 90 percent of the Western U.S.—not to mention threatening the water supply of several major cities and western aquifers.

On an even larger scale, snow and ice reflect most of the solar radiation that hits them, while simultaneously acting as a heat sink that cools the atmosphere. When they melt, a feedback kicks in. Less reflectivity means more of the sun's heat is absorbed into dark land and water, and the planet warms faster—in turn, melting more snow and ice. The 8.8

million square miles of permafrost in the Northern Hemisphere, which traps much of the planet's methane and carbon, also has a feedback loop. When it melts, those greenhouse gases are released, accelerating global warming even more. Lastly, because fresh water from melting snow and ice decreases the salinity of the ocean, altering large currents like the thermohaline circulation in the North Atlantic, global weather patterns change and the way that snow and rain are distributed around the world changes with them. So vanishing snow is fueling the Great Melt, and the more momentum warming gains, the less humans have the ability to stop it.

Armstrong is quick to point out that every climate model contains a margin of error. The basic warming trend has been proven and will continue for some time, he says. Discerning where snow and rain will fall is a trickier game that climatologists are just getting their heads around. "If you look at 20 different models of climate prediction, you've got a plot without a lot of scatter," he says. "If you do the same models with precip, there's no agreement whatsoever. Because they haven't figured out how to handle clouds....Precipitation patterns depend on whether fewer or more clouds are generated from that process. But they don't quite have a handle on that."

One side effect he's more confident about, as a backcountry skier and longtime snow scientist, is that there will be more winter-weather anomalies like rain-on-snow events, intense storms and longer periods between storms. All of those things increase avalanche danger—altering how we travel in the backcountry, not to mention on mountain highways. Like many other aspects of climate change these days, this is less speculation than observation. Because it's already happening.

Chapter Five

The Man with Three First Names

Ski bums are ski bums and they always will be…

—*Opening line,* Soul Sessions and Epic Impressions, *MSP, 1993*

When the man with three first names wasn't skiing the Cascades, he was scheming a way to get back there. Jim Norman Jack grew up in Redmond, east of Seattle, and graduated in 1984 from Lakes High School in Tacoma. He visited his grandparents' cabin on Lake Wenatchee often, and when it came time to go to college, he chose Central Washington University, an hour south of Wenatchee on U.S. 97.

The 46-year-old was the kind of man who had nicknames for everyone, and everyone had one for him: Stormin' Norman, J.J., Jimmy Jam, The Mayor of Mission Ridge, The Mayor of Alta, The Grandfather of Freeskiing, Superman. He had a sandwich named after him in a pub in Leavenworth, down the street from the bungalow he lived in with Tiffany Abraham.

Above all things, Jack was a Northwesterner. In the winter his beard was usually cemented with snow. He loved to drink beer, and he had that calm and fair way about him that people who live slightly closer to the heavens often do. Pacific Northwest skiers are a different breed. It might be the isolation of living in the corner pocket of America, or maybe the fact that they can ski fresh powder practically every time they step out their door. Good snow can spoil a man, and keep him close to home. Which is probably why no matter where Jack went, he always gravitated back to the Cascades.

He worked forestry jobs in the summers, fighting fires, shuttling firefighters and running a program that put inmates to work in the woods. He had a way of inspiring people, lifting them up and giving them the confidence to do things they otherwise wouldn't have tried. He was a great influence on the inmates in the USFS program and was so good with a chainsaw, his friends could place a beer can in the woods and Jack would fell a tree on it.

Jack was a young man with an old soul, perhaps from knowing so early on what he was put on Earth to do. He stood a solid 5 foot 11, had sandy brown hair, a Roman nose and a close-cropped beard with a patch of gray under the chin. His face was scored with a perpetual goggle tan and his raspy voice sounded like he'd stayed up late the night before, which was often the case. He wore his emotions on his sleeve and his expression seemed to teeter on the brink of a smile. When he did his whole face reacted, with crow's feet crowding his blue eyes and deep dimples growing in his cheeks.

When Jack's college professors said it was time to pick a career, he chose a ski-resort management program at Wenatchee Valley College, 12 miles down the road from Mission Ridge Ski Resort. WVC and a few other colleges in the West started resort-management programs in the 1980s—in part as a solution for young ski bums looking to earn a college degree while skiing seven days a week. The Mission Ridge scene—a six-lift ma-and-pa resort set on the eastern edge of the Cascades—was one to behold back then. WVC classes met on the hill, and every weekday 200 students hell-bent on skiing for the rest of their lives barnstormed the mountain. They ripped bump lines under the chairlift, flashed the rocky chutes above Bomber Bowl and on weekends headed up the road to Stevens Pass.

Two young skiers, Murray Wais and Steve Winter, entered the WVC ski-instruction program a year before Jack. The pair would go on to make some of the most iconic ski films of the last two decades with their company, Matchstick Productions. In 1988 they were still starry-eyed college kids obsessed with powder. Wais had heard of Jack's skiing prowess while attending a rival high school in Tacoma, and the two hooked up immediately. Their ski posse called itself "The Shred Crew" and made T-shirts with the slogan "Ski or Die" set against a silhouette of their hero, Scot Schmidt, and a Grateful Dead graphic. Two years later, after immersing in the camaraderie of skiing with friends every day, whooping at each other from the lift and pushing themselves to go bigger and faster, Jack graduated from WVC with what had become his second family—one that he'd live with for the rest of his life.

During his time at WVC, Winter bought a movie camera and a few rolls of film. He was inspired by Greg Stump's *The Blizzard of Aahhh's* and filmed Jack skiing around the mountain and leaping off cliffs into deep Cascadian powder. The film was Winter's first and he sent it to K2 to get funding for a full-length movie. When K2 gave him the thumbs-up, he packed up shop, rented a house in Crested Butte and headed south to make *Soul Sessions and Epic Impressions*. Opening line: "Ski bums are ski bums and they always will be…"

The thing about skiers is that the better they get, the more conditions, mountains and slopes they want to try. So when Winter headed to Colorado to start filming, Jack tagged along and spent the winter skiing the Rockies. He ended up working more as a producer on the film than a skier, but the experience opened his eyes to the 14,000-foot peaks of Colorado. After a few seasons working at Alpental and Crystal, he made his way south again, this time to Alta.

Jack chased powder at Alta for a season before hooking up with Rob Castillo. He worked at the Top of the Lodge Restaurant, then as a wine steward at the Alta Lodge. He entered the Freeskiing World Tour's first competitions in Crested Butte and Snowbird, with Castillo and Dave McReynolds. By the time he left Alta, eight years later, he was 36 years old, one of the best freeskiers in the country and had become a recognized name in the burgeoning freeskiing movement.

After shattering his orbital socket with his knee in a competition, Jack turned to the administrative side of events. He began judging contests for the FWT and served as IFSA president for a year. He helped create a universal line-item judging system for the tour and merge the FWT with the European Freeride World Tour—and eventually became the FWT head judge.

The winter of 2011–2012 had been a difficult season for the FWT. The Crested Butte event and several others were canceled due to lack of snow, and still others were moved to new venues. Jack was paid per event, and with paychecks few and far between he drove to Crystal Mountain in February to work for a sister event called The North Face Masters of Snowboarding. Keith Carlsen was producing a webcast of the competition and, when it was over, asked Jack for a ride to Stevens—where he was headed to shoot the *Powder* feature on night-skiing. That afternoon the two loaded their gear into Jack's '97 Chevy Silverado and took off down WA-410 on the four-hour drive.

About 12 hours before, a high-pressure system over the Cascades broke down and a southerly flow delivered the area's first precipitation in more than two weeks. The last major storm at the end of January doused the mountains with rain all the way to the top of Cowboy Ridge. The clear, cold nights that followed formed a thick rain crust over Stevens's slopes. Crusts are loath to skiers for a few reasons. They make skiing backcountry or ungroomed runs almost impossible, as the crust grabs the edge, tip and tail of the ski, making it incredibly difficult to turn. More importantly, though, the crust facilitates the formation of invisible weak layers in the snowpack that skiers can unknowingly trigger.

To make matters worse, a coating of feathery surface hoar spread across the slopes of Stevens Pass during the clear nights of February 3–7.

Surface hoar is similar to the frost that grows on a car windshield at night and is a booby trap of sorts. It is difficult to detect, strong enough to be buried for months at a time and, when it's loaded with new snow, it can collapse, often under a skier's weight.

Carlsen and Jack's conversation wasn't about avalanches, though, as they drove past Redmond, crossed the Skykomish River and approached the Stevens Pass Highway. It was about the snowflakes whooshing over the windshield and which runs to hit first the next day. Jack's brakes had a penchant for locking up, and the drive took a little longer than usual. Around 8:00 p.m. they finally saw the glow of Stevens's night-skiing lights and pulled into the RV lot.

Jack, Carlsen and John Stifter, who was there to write the story Carlsen was shooting, skied the next day and into the night. It was snowing hard by then and Carlsen set up shots of Jack, Tim Wangen and John Brenan plunging into the gathering powder. High above, a low-pressure trough had developed and brought loads of moisture off the Pacific with it. Freezing levels dropped from 8,000 feet to around 2,000, setting up what looked to be an epically light powder day for Stevens on Sunday. There was a foot and a half of snow on top of the RVs by the time the group made it to the bonfire. Abraham hadn't seen Jack in a week and they soon left to cozy up in the Vacationeer. In the morning, Abraham woke early to give a massage in Leavenworth. Jack was exhausted from the trip and slept in longer. When he finally woke up, there was almost two feet of new snow on the ground. He gathered his gear and closed up the camper, then trudged up the hill to get in line for the lift.

An avalanche starts weeks, sometimes months, before it careens down a mountainside. As layers of snow pile up—often of different density, temperature, hardness and crystal type—gravity pulls them downhill, slowly stressing and deforming weak layers in the snowpack. The strain resulting from the weight and settling of the snowpack can cause the bonds between certain layers to fail. Depending on conditions like temperature, which can affect the rate of settling, failure of a weak layer can occur as gradually as a few centimeters per hour. If disturbed by a skier, a fracture can rip horizontally at 200 miles per hour.

No two avalanches are the same and no two slopes are the same either. The angle of the slope varies, as does exposure to the sun, wind-loading and skier compaction. On some parts of a slope a deposit of new snow can be thinner than on others, allowing more of a skier's weight to transfer to the weak layer. In other places the weak layer is bonded more poorly, meaning avalanches aren't always triggered by the first skier to schuss down the slope. Slides often release on the 3rd, 5th or 12th skier. Avalanche scientists call the zone that is most apt to fracture "the sweet spot." And it can be located just 10 feet to the right or left of a skier's tracks.

It was the seventh skier on his third turn that triggered the February 19 slide at Tunnel Creek. The fracture zipped 200 feet across the slope, initially sliding on the layer of surface hoar that collapsed. It then stepped down to the slick rain crust. The mass of snow accelerated to 20 miles per hour within the first three seconds. Five seconds later, around the time it hit the trees where Castillo, Rudolph, Brenan and Saugstad were standing, it was a 25-foot-tall, million-plus-pound wall of snow, ice and air hurtling at more than 50 miles per hour.

The impact it made when it hit the trees is similar to that of a tidal wave rushing onshore: a churning wall of liquid mass that sweeps everything in its path away. The slide ripped the bark off trees, snapped other trees in half and tore up rocks from the ground. The friction from ice crystals colliding into one another elevated the temperature of the slide a few degrees and scored the icy walls of the Tunnel Creek drainage.

By the time the avalanche hit Castillo, he'd wrapped his arms around both of the trees he was standing above. The slide thrashed the avalanche shovel strapped to his pack as he tried to hold on, millions of pounds of debris trying to rip him away. Physics and a century of avalanche science say it would have been impossible for him to hold on. Castillo's helmet cam captured 21 seconds of whitewash before, slowly, the snow began to subside. He thought about shooting a hand up in the air to signal rescuers in case he was buried. But the snow soon flowed around his shoulders, then dropped to his knees and, eventually, his boots. Somehow his skis had stayed on; miraculously, he was uninjured. He pushed back from the trees and freed his legs, euphoric, terrified and in shock.

He wasn't sure what had happened at first. The landscape around him was foreign. The sublime powder scene of 30 seconds ago, with sparkling crystals, friends smiling and hoots of joy, had been replaced by a war zone. Some of the group had skied a different way down and might be safe; others were likely still standing at the top. Everyone who had been in the trees with Castillo was gone.

The only sound he could make out was the creak of old-growth spruce as the trees recoiled from being bent over. A fine mist of crystals from the powder blast settled on his shoulders. He screamed for Brenan and the others. No response. It was like the hand of God, in half a minute, had swept every living thing from the forest.

When Castillo looked downhill at the carnage in Tunnel Creek, stretching more than 2,000 vertical feet, he realized what had happened. He immediately switched his avalanche beacon to "search." The beacons are standard backcountry gear, along with a probe and shovel to find and dig people out. Everyone in the group had been wearing one. The beacons broadcast a radio signal, so people who aren't caught in a slide can turn theirs to search mode and find the ones who were. The closer the beeps sound together, the closer a skier is to finding his or her friend. The farther apart, the lower the friend's chances of survival. In the frightening and chaotic scene following an avalanche, the transceivers often determine whether someone lives or dies.

The drainage below was steep and tight and had been scoured to blue ice. The high-banked walls and cliff bands were impossible to navigate. Castillo instead traversed skier's left to find Wangen and Peikert, who had watched the avalanche from the safety of a ridge. Peikert was still traversing off the slope when the slide rushed behind him and crossed his tracks.

"[Wangen, Peikert and I] worked our way down, and at a certain point I realized, 'Fuck, they're not up here,'" Castillo recalls. "They're down. So we started moving down. I found Johnny's ski up in a tree, about three and a half feet. At that point, something told me we were on body recovery. I called 911 and told the other guys to get down there, keep searching. They overtook me because I made that phone call, and I got cliffed out because I was trying to stay out of that gully. It was gnarly. It was 10 feet high and carved out—two icy runnels."

When Castillo got to the bottom, Tim Carlson and Ron Pankey were already searching near the foot of the avalanche deposition zone. They'd skied high on the ridgeline, following the tracks of another member of the group. They were the first ones on the scene, about 10 minutes after the slide deposited a football-field-wide swath of debris. After 15 minutes, survival of buried avalanche victims drops to 40 percent. Several others from the group—including Stifter, Dan Abrams and Megan Michelson—had searched the slide path from the top of the run and were finishing a beacon search at the bottom when Castillo arrived.

"I got to them and was like 'Right here, he's buried right here,'" he recalls. "They had a shovel and a probe out already. Everyone was pretty on it. Right then Wenzel said, 'I got something. I need a digger.' I left those guys. I told them to dig. And I went and started digging with Wenzel. Then I saw the backpack, saw the red-and-black helmet, and I knew it was Johnny."

John Brenan was built as tough as they come, but being hurtled 2,000 feet down a vertical mountainside was too much. It took a while to chip Brenan's entombed body out of the snow, and when they did it was completely broken. His helmet had been pushed to the back of his head and was filled with snow. His leg was bent at an odd angle and he had a gash on his chin.

Castillo and Peikert performed CPR. Castillo knew his old friend and ski buddy was probably gone, but he also knew that Brenan's wife and kids were waiting for him at the bottom. When they stopped CPR 30 minutes later, Castillo sat down in shock. He'd skied hundreds of runs with Brenan. He'd worked for him and spent time with his daughters. The thought that a powder run had killed him was surreal. On the coroner's report, there was no single cause of death other than blunt trauma to the entire body.

Just above Brenan, Saugstad had been partially buried. When the slide engulfed her, she'd inflated her emergency-airbag backpack, built to float a skier to the top of the debris in the event of an avalanche. She'd tumbled down the entire mountain in a maelstrom of white, miraculously missing all of the obstacles, and came to rest in the debris. Only her head and hands were free. Her nose ring had been torn off. The rest of her body was cemented in the snow. The whole episode lasted less than a minute. Peikert dug her out just before digging for Brenan.

Above her, Stifter, Abrams and Wangen searched for another victim Peikert had marked with his pole. The lowest reading Stifter got on his beacon was 2.4 meters, meaning the skier was buried more than seven feet down. They chipped away at the ice and found Chris Rudolph facedown. It took a while to get his feet free, then they pulled him out and administered CPR. Rudolph's face was already blue, and he never responded.

Down below, the scene was morbid. Skiers wandered over giant chunks of snow and ice; bodies lay on the ground. Crystals from the powder blast were still settling and a thin fog shrouded the slope. Pankey was tracking a signal and Castillo went to help him. Pankey mentioned that Jim Jack was down below. At that point, Castillo didn't know that Jack had been in the slide.

Pankey told Castillo that Jack was gone, and Castillo looked at him in disbelief. Jack was the great pacifier, the Peter Pan of Never-Never Land. He couldn't be gone. He went to his friend's body to give him CPR but soon realized that it was over. Jack had been the seventh skier. His third turn was over the sweet spot that triggered the avalanche.

Years of friendship, skiing, road-tripping, girlfriends and shenanigans played out in an instant. The two had skied the greatest mountains of North America together, pioneered first descents and entered a tier of the sport that few ever see. But the great arc of Jack's life—from high school to Mission Ridge to Alta and back to his homeland—ended here. Castillo hugged his friend and pulled Jack's hood over his head. Then he said goodbye to the man with three first names for the last time.

Chapter Six

The Signal and the Response

If the sea is always advancing in one place and receding in another it is clear that the same parts of the whole earth are not always either sea or land, but that all this changes in course of time.

—*Aristotle,* Meteorologica, *340 BC*

Before the 20th century, models to predict the weather were based on astrology and myth. Babylonians in the sixth century BC forecasted weather by interpreting cloud patterns. Aztec kings sacrificed humans to coax the rain god, Tloloc, to water their fields. Aristotle came closest to the mark in his 340 BC text *Meteorologica*, with his theory that weather arose from the interaction of fire, air, land and water. Later, his student, Theophrastus, went further in *On Signs*, explaining how to interpret halos, the color of the sky and even "sounds" to predict storms.

It wasn't until the early 1900s that scientists developed more precise methods. In 1904, Norwegian physicist Vilhelm Bjerknes created a two-step technique—diagnostic and prognostic—to calculate current weather conditions and predict them in the future. Englishman Lewis Fry Richardson took the research further in 1922, attempting to retro-actively predict the weather on May 20, 1910, in two areas in Europe. His calculations, done by hand, took six days to compute and were significantly inaccurate, though his process formed the basis for modern weather prediction.

It took a 100-foot-long, 30-ton military computer to bring about the modern era of weather forecasting. Meteorology was ahead of the computer curve at that time and the Army's ENIAC computer—designed to calculate artillery firing tables—required 24 hours to make a 24-hour forecast. As computer speeds accelerated in the 1960s and '70s—and meteorologists added inputs for things like solar radiation, moisture effects and, eventually, variables like the extent of sea ice—the age of global weather forecasting arrived.

Simultaneously, scientists tried to get their heads around predicting climate—defined as the average of weather calculated over several decades. The first climate models were grand in scale, analyzing the general circulation of the atmosphere. They gradually tightened in scope and accuracy, adding inputs for land surface and the ocean. After global warming was identified—and NASA devised instruments and satellites to analyze it—researchers devised models to gauge carbon content and atmospheric chemistry.

Global models require vast amounts of data collected all over the world to approach any kind of accuracy. After politicians recognized the imminent danger climate change poses, the first large-scale international collaborations on modeling began. When the Intergovernmental Panel on Climate Change was created in 1988, the initial scientific assessment of Work Group 1 was this: "Improved prediction of climate change depends on the development of climate models, which is the objective of the climate modeling programme of the World Climate Research Programme." The ultimate goal: read the future.

Sometime in the 1990s one of the first industries to be affected by climate change in the U.S. started looking around for someone to read *their* future. Set between the low-slung Mayacamas and Vaca mountains, just south of the 40th parallel in Northern California, Napa Valley has long been known as the premium wine-growing region in America. When a Napa Valley chardonnay and cabernet sauvignon won blind taste tests at the Paris Wine Tasting of 1976, the world was stunned—and Northern

California took its place among the most vaunted wine-growing areas in the world.

It wasn't just soil and tending that allowed Napa vintners to beat the great Mediterranean vineyards. It was the Mediterranean climate itself. Along with a half dozen swaths of land scattered across Australia, South Africa, Chile and Central Asia, Napa Valley enjoys almost the exact same climate as the great wine-producing regions of Europe: hot, dry summers and cool, wet winters. Seasonal high-pressure cells, which move toward the poles in the summer and toward the equator in the winter, create the conditions. And, like every other region on Earth, the areas are being significantly affected by climate change.

In 2006, a study funded by the Purdue Climate Change Research Center asserted that climate change could reduce wine production in the $2.9 billion U.S. market by 81 percent by 2100. Dr. Noah Diffenbaugh co-authored the 2006 study and in 2011 headed up another on a tighter, more regional scale. Until recently, scientists had been capable of predicting climate change only on a global level, 75 to 100 years out. Diffenbaugh, and handful of other scientists around the world, have been changing that as of late.

The model that Diffenbaugh and his colleagues created had 25 kilometers of horizontal resolution—four times higher detail than most global models—and included factors like coastal wind speeds and ocean temperatures. The team input historical data collected between 1960 and 2010 and compared results to historical observations. The model came out with more than 90 percent accuracy. Its conclusion: the area suitable for premium wine-grape production in California could be reduced over the next 30 years by as much as 50 percent in some counties.[15]

Diffenbaugh's next project, published in the journal *Nature Climate Change* in November 2012, was a prediction of snowpack extent in the Northern Hemisphere. Part of the study on the wine industry focused on weather extremes (e.g., record hot summers), and he and co-authors Moetasim Ashfaq and Martin Scherer followed a similar approach in the snow study. One of the main claims of "Response of snow-dependent hydrologic extremes to continued global warming" was that if temperatures rise 3.6 degrees Fahrenheit—as they are predicted to do by mid-century—30 percent of winters in the Northern Hemisphere will bring seasonal snowfall below current record low levels. By 2070, the paper says, low snow years will be the norm more than 80 percent of the time. In plain English, this means the winter drought that used to happen once every 15 years will soon start to happen about every three.

Diffenbaugh is a rock star in the world of climate change, appearing on TV news programs alongside Al Gore and quoted in practically every major news outlet in the country. He continued to Stanford after Purdue, where he is now the assistant professor in the Department of Environmental Earth System Science. He has the good looks of a soap opera star playing the role of a scientist on TV: perfect center part in his wavy brown hair, a quiver of open-collar button-downs with a different color for every occasion. In interviews his voice has the slow cadence of a college professor, not so much relaxed as it is precise.

One of the most alarming trends Diffenbaugh reports in the paper is that the Western U.S. shows both the earliest emergence of frequent extremely low snow years and the largest occurrence of extremely low snow years in the study. Previously scientists had predicted that the high elevation and low temperatures of interior high-alpine ranges, like those in Colorado, would be somewhat immune to climate change in the near term. But Diffenbaugh's study saw otherwise.

"The key result in these analyses is the dominance of temperature," he says, "how the warming overwhelms any effect that we found in changes in precipitation. So whether the models agree on precipitation or not, whether they agree on the location of storms or not, the temperature increase is so large and so robust across the different models that the response of spring snow accumulation, the response of the timing and amount of snowfall runoff, is very strong.

"There certainly will continue to be snow in the world. The question is really how much of the precipitation is snow, when it falls and how long does it stay on the ground before it melts. These models are in agreement that even with another degree of Celsius of global warming, which is relatively moderate from the perspective of international policy negotiations, even *that* causes substantial areas of the Northern Hemisphere to experience increasing occurrences of extremely low snow years, extremely high winter runoff and extremely low spring and summer runoff."

Climate models have come a long way since ENIAC, thanks largely to increased computer speed. The more precise and sophisticated they get, the more they agree on overall climate change projections—like how the poles are heating faster than the rest of the planet, and the expected northward expansion of arid conditions around the 30th parallel north. When it comes to snow and skiing, though, there is room for discrepancy, Daniel Scott says. According to his numbers, there is a good chance that snow and skiing will fare just fine in a warmer world.

Scott holds the Canada Research Chair in Global Change and Tourism at the University of Waterloo in Ontario. When it comes to climate models and skiing, he is not one to pull his punches. He co-authored the report "Managing for Climate Change in the Alpine Ski Sector," which spelled the coming end of more than half of the ski resorts in the Northeast in the next 30 years. The University of Waterloo was one of the first institutions to investigate the relationship between climate change and skiing, in the 1980s. Many of the computer models used in Europe today came from the university. Scott built his own model 10 years ago and has been using it ever since to predict what will happen to skiing in the next century.

One detail that skiers and the media often miss, he says, is that most snow studies to date have been done from a hydrology perspective. Papers like Diffenbaugh's take a broad approach and try to discern how much water will come out of the system in the spring, for farms and reservoirs, rather than how much snow is on the ground every day of the winter. As a result, many of the conclusions have less to do with skiing than with the climate's effect on year-round water supply. While hydrological research is essential to affected regions like California—which could face an agricultural collapse if snow disappears—it is misleading in terms of where there will and will not be skiing.

"How much snowpack is there on April 1?" Scott asks. "Well, that's great to know in terms of how much water is going to be available, but it means nothing to the ski industry. Skiers need to know what fell in November and December....We looked at how they did the study that came out of the University of Colorado and went, 'What the heck?' This has no relevance to the ski industry. They were saying the amount of snowpack in April was cut in half, but it was still being measured in meters. In most places if it's four meters and you cut it in half, that's still plenty for skiing. Some of the things that have been talked about in the past, they shouldn't have been saying some of the things they were. That's partly why we applied our model to the Vail context."

Rather than rely on specific climate models, Scott and his team created what he calls a "sensitivity analysis." The program runs 52 scenarios where the climate can be warmer or colder, with less or more precipitation. They then plug in various global climate projections and see what it means for a given ski area's season, length, opening day and snowpack. The last measure that Scott added to the analysis, and others leave out, is a snowmaking module. Based on interviews with dozens of ski-area executives, when conditions allow, the module inputs manmade snow into the equation.

"Our study out there found very different results from what has been reported in much of the media," Scott says. "Colorado, under some of the warmer scenarios that were available, at least through mid-century as long as snowmaking was in place, was quite viable. Some shrinkage in season, but not a lot."

Scott's analysis comes up with many of the same bleak prognostications for coastal resorts, but his research suggests that many resorts in the Rockies will likely fare just fine, as long as they have snowmaking coverage across the mountain. Vail is one of the lowest-elevation resorts—and thus most affected by climate change—but by Scott's calculations it would still be able to maintain a 100-plus-day season in up to a 6 degrees Celsius increase in temperature. (Most models predict the Colorado climate will climb about 4 degrees Celsius by 2050.) With a 6 degrees Celsius spike, snowmaking requirements would have to increase between 59 and 94 percent to keep the mountain open and commercially viable. That could be challenging with dwindling water supplies expected, but not impossible, Scott points out, considering that many snowmaking systems recycle the water that they put on the hill.

Not worrying that spring snowpack has been cut in half, because there's plenty of snow to ski on, doesn't seem prudent in the face of climate change. Especially if coming decades will see it reduced by half again. The reality is, people living and recreating in the mountains— similar to polar bears and vintners—will soon be among the first to see climate change radically alter their world. They are the canaries in the coal mine. What advocates trying to save snow are hoping is that, as an affluent, influential and international community 65 million strong, snow sports enthusiasts are incentivized enough by what they see to become one of the first major civilian sectors to do something about it.

The growing sentiment that global warming is a forgone conclusion— and the hesitancy of the skiing world, and the world at large, to react to it—is Scott's final contention. Humans had a significant hand in warming the Earth; they can have one in stopping that trend too, he says. All it takes is cutting greenhouse gas emissions. Which, in turn, takes legislation and enforcement. Which takes world leaders putting their foot down— something, so far, they've led the public to believe is impossible.

But if they could, Scott says, it would be conceivable to slow warming down by several degrees. Instead of a 6 degrees Celsius spike in the next 100 years, decimating the snowpack in the Northern Hemisphere and propelling the world into economic and environmental turmoil, warming could be held to the U.N.-mandated 2 degrees Celsius limit—and we could ski into the 22nd century.

"From a skiing perspective, a 2 degrees Celsius increase is a very different world than if we approach plus-4 degrees Celsius or plus-5 degrees Celsius," Scott says. "I look around me at a lot of smart people who are doing a heck of a lot of innovation, and I think across Canada, across the United States, across the world. I think if the conditions are put in place, whether it be policy or simply put a price on carbon and make a market for it, you'll have a lot of bright businesspeople and scientists putting their heads together, and it will get solved. Someone said we need a Manhattan Project–type approach to renewable energy, and I think if the U.S. or some other big countries did that, definitely it will be solved by mid-century."

An 80 percent cut in emissions could keep global warming to a 3 degrees Celsius rise, which would mean slower melting of sea ice, less desalination of the oceans, less disruption of global weather patterns and less displacement of people, agriculture and civilization. In the high peaks of the Sierra Nevada and the ridgelines of the North Cascades, it would mean feathery snow instead of rain falling—which would allow skiers to slip through cold smoke every day of the winter. It is a dream that seems worth fighting for, Scott says, and one that millions of skiers around the world should know is attainable.

Chapter Seven

The Beginning

Mountains will crumble, but the emptiness of space, which is the one universal essence of mind, the vast awakenerhood, empty and awake, will never crumble away because it was never born.

—*Jack Kerouac*

Mid-February is high season in the mountains, and Joel Martinez was either in meetings or putting out fires from his office on the third floor of the Tye Creek Lodge on February 19. Martinez arrived at Stevens Pass 13 years ago as a skier, but now wears the hat of vice president of operations. He has the look of a Pacific Northwest skier, with an athletic build, carpenter's hands and the kind of demure seriousness that makes him look away when he smiles. He grew up in Tahoe and at first didn't know what to make of the small-town Stevens scene: bushy beards, beater pickup trucks, the trailer-park vibe in the RV lot. When the resort received 500 inches of snow his first winter—and everyone said it was a bad year—he decided to stay.

Martinez is one of those gifted skiers capable of straddling the line between doing the thing he loves and paying the bills at the same time. He and Chris Rudolph skied together every day, and when Martinez was busy Rudolph skied with Martinez's kids. They worked closely together, managed Kehr's Cabin and shared a deep love for the town and mountain they'd stumbled across. They weren't getting rich; they did it for other reasons—mainly skiing, serving their adopted community and promoting the resort they were both proud to call their home hill.

Martinez describes Rudolph as the kind of marketing guy who hated marketing guys. "He made connections through relationships," he says, "sometimes taking up to three years to convince someone to come to Stevens." Rudolph was also a transplant from Northern California who'd fallen in love with the Pacific Northwest. He facetiously called Colorado "Call Me Rad Bro." He was generous and kind, a motivator who brought people together and made great things happen. One of his favorite sayings was, "Be the person your dog thinks you are."

Martinez knew Jim Jack and John Brenan as well. Jack had been an unofficial ambassador for Stevens Pass for years, singing its praises and luring pros, photographers and cinematographers to the resort. He conceived of and appeared in an Internet video promoting the town of Leavenworth, featuring nutcracker Woody Goomsba in a faux music video complete with a cast of four sexy dancers. "Off the Couch Johnny" Brenan had also been a friend for years. Whether he was running a construction site in town or hitting the community Leavenworth Ski Hill, where his daughters skied and raced, Brenan was always up for an adventure. One race day on the road, Martinez remembers, he shared a beer with Brenan at 8:00 a.m. while their kids whizzed through the racing gates. Martinez's wife asked him what he was doing, to which he replied, "It's Johnny!" And everything was OK.

As vice president of operations, Martinez was in charge of just about everything on the mountain February 19: concessions, chairlifts, parking, safety. With 5,000 skiers on the hill that day, he was annoyed at first when Rudolph asked him if he would pick up the Tunnel Creek crew at the bottom of their run. Martinez tore a ligament in his knee while skiing with Rudolph in 2011 and was still rehabbing. He knew that big powder days were a big reason why he and Rudolph coveted their jobs, and in the end—even though he was going stir-crazy in the office—he was happy Rudolph could get a run in. So around noon Martinez let the phones ring in his office and drove the Stevens Pass passenger van to the turnout on Highway 2 to wait for the group.

It was a while before Martinez heard chatter about an accident on his two-way radio. He didn't pay attention at first. He was away from his desk and figured the ski patrol could handle any situation on the mountain until he returned. Then an ambulance pulled up behind him. Then a state trooper. Martinez asked what was going on and the trooper said that there'd been an avalanche. Martinez asked where. "Tunnel Creek," the trooper said.

"I knew the odds were against me then," Martinez says. "There were eight people missing at that point, and I probably knew at least one of them." Martinez drove back to the resort immediately. There, controlled chaos was beginning to unfold. Skiers and patrollers milled around the ski patrol shack. He saw Tiffany Abraham and Rudolph's girlfriend, Anne Hessburg, sitting inside. A patroller approached Martinez and told him that his friend and colleague Chris Rudolph was dead. Then that Jim Jack had been killed as well. Martinez stood in a daze, unsure what to do or say—or who to go to now that his right-hand man was inexplicably gone. His cell phone was already ringing nonstop. "*The New York Times*, CNN, everyone was calling," he recalls. "I have no idea how they even got my number. There were still thousands of skiers on the hill and the resort had to open in the morning. We had no marketing contact anymore, so the CEO and I sat down and planned what to say to the press."

Martinez's wife was one of the callers trying to get through. She knew if her husband's knee was feeling up to it, he might have tagged along for a quick powder run between meetings. He called her back and she told him that his kids wanted to see him. When he finally saw them that night, his daughter told him that she was happy his knee was hurt. She knew he would have been skiing Tunnel Creek if he was healthy. She was right, Martinez says. He might even have had his son in tow.

After sending more patrollers to help, then a D.O.T. snowcat to collect the bodies, Martinez drove the van back to the turnout. When he arrived, a patroller told him that John Brenan had died too. It was too much for anyone to process. Not just one, but three of the pillars of Stevens Pass had been swept away in less than a minute. It seemed cruel, the end of an era, and that's exactly what it was. The group hadn't been out to make a first descent; they weren't competing or filming on a death-defying slope. They were young, but not young and dumb. They were just a bunch of friends taking a lunchtime powder run that they'd skied many, many times before. It was the run that they would have talked about around the fire in the RV lot that night.

Laurie Brenan, Hessburg and Abraham were all in the ski patrol shack when they got the news. Abraham and Brenan had wandered there from the Bull's Tooth Pub, where someone had mentioned that there'd been an avalanche in Tunnel Creek. Hessburg was storing her skis in Kehr's Cabin when a friend got the call. It was the unenviable job of patrol manager Chris Brixey to relay the bad news. Rescuers had tried to revive them, but their men were gone.

Back on the slope, rescuers stood vigil around the bodies. There was nothing more that could be done. The ski patrol told the other skiers in the group to catch a ride back to the mountain in the ambulance, but Stifter and Carlsen stayed, partly in shock, partly feeling that there must be something else they could do.

The rescue effort was officially called off shortly thereafter and snowmobiles arrived from down valley, along with a second shift of patrollers to transport the bodies. They wrapped the three men in blankets and loaded them onto the cat. Martinez waited at the bottom, wanting to be the last man out, wanting to ensure no one else got hurt. He was sitting in the van when the snowcat returned to the highway. It was then that the gravity of the catastrophe hit. His friends were gone, taken by a single crystal that gave way to a million others. Their bodies now lay on the back of the snowcat. He could tell who was who by the ski boots still on their feet.

One of the grim duties of working for a ski magazine is being on the front lines of bad news. I was sitting at my desk at *Powder* in California in 2001 when I got word that 30-year-old ski mountaineer Hans Saari had fallen to his death in Chamonix. Saari was a prodigy, one of the most talented young mountaineers I'd ever seen. I'd met him in Peru, where we were both climbing and skiing in the Cordillera Blanca. He was a gentleman beyond his years who skied "proud lines" and used words like "sporty." He was a good writer, too, and was on assignment for me, skiing the Gervasutti Couloir, when he slipped on black ice and fell to his death. That summer I flew to Bozeman, Montana, to meet his family and attend his memorial. My only piece of luggage was a framed portrait of Saari that *Powder* photo editor David Reddick had printed to give to his grieving parents.

I was working at another desk when Aaron Martin and Reid Sanders died on Mount Saint Elias a year later. I remember exactly where I was when I heard about Carl Skoog, Billy Poole and Shane McConkey, all taken by the mountains. I had just skipped a heli-ski trip in Alaska and absconded to my aunt's house on Long Island to finish a manuscript when I learned that Doug Coombs had fallen to his death in the Alps. I'd written my first skiing stories about Doug in the 1990s, published his first articles in my 'zine, *The Pass*, and written my first magazine feature, in 1997, about his heli-ski operation in Valdez. One of the highlights of my skiing career was smoking a joint with Coombs while straddling a knife-edge col 12,000 feet up on Wyoming's Middle Teton, then skiing down behind him.

I won't recount the dozens of stories that were published and aired after the Tunnel Creek avalanche. I will say that most reporters overtly or subtly hinted at mistakes that were made and lessons that could be learned—most of which are true. But the line was drawn when reporters and editors started the inevitable search for blame. As most everyone at Tunnel Creek that day agrees, mistakes were made. There was too much new snow to not exercise vigilant backcountry protocol. The group was too big. The avalanche report and snowpack history were too dangerous to be ignored. The thing the media missed—because most penning the articles were not skiers and not familiar with that environment—is the fact that there is no black and white when you're traveling in the wilderness. Thousands of mistakes and misjudgments are made in the mountains every year and the groups ski away unscathed. There is always risk, so probability plays a role. Sometimes you simply do the wrong thing in the wrong place at the wrong time.

"Even as a kid, I knew each run could be it," Rob Castillo told me a year after the accident. "I don't know if I've ever been comfortable with that, but I was willing to accept it and take the risk anyway. You hear people saying [in reaction to the stories published on Tunnel Creek] that 'I've been skiing 20 years and I've never done something like that.' And I'm like, really? How many times did you get lucky and you don't even know how lucky you got? One foot to the right and you hit the pocket…"

The media storm that followed the accident was unprecedented in skiing history. Hundreds of phone calls and emails from around the country poured in, all trying to get the scoop on what happened. *The New York Times* ran a story titled "Avalanches on the Rise for Thrill-Seeking Skiers," which pointed out that avalanche deaths in the U.S. were projected to be "a little higher" in the 2011-2012 winter than the national average of 28.8. The total ended up being 34—a difference of five people in a field of thousands—14 of whom were snowmobilers or hikers. *The Huffington Post* followed with "Avalanche Deaths on the Rise This Season, but Why?," then the *Los Angeles Times* with "Deaths Caused by Avalanches on the Rise."

The night of the accident, Elyse Saugstad taped an interview for *Good Morning America* and *Today* about surviving the slide. Megan Michelson accompanied her to help deal with the frenzy. One caller, an angry producer at *Good Morning America,* lectured Michelson for not giving his show an exclusive on Saugstad's interview. "You have no idea what a war zone morning television is," he said. Michelson would later write a revealing and sincere 4,000-word account of the accident in *Outside* magazine called "Tunnel Vision." John Branch followed with one of the longest stories ever published in *The New York Times,* a 17,000-word multimedia special report that meticulously recreated the day from start to finish, including graphics and videos about avalanche science, powder skiing and testimonials from survivors. The story, "Snow Fall:

The Avalanche at Tunnel Creek," was published almost a year after the accident and won a 2013 Pulitzer Prize.

While the national media wrangled with the ideas of risk, regulation and liability regarding avalanches in North America, they missed a surprising trend. Mark Moore, the avalanche forecaster who made the report for Stevens Pass on February 19, 2012, pointed it out: global weather patterns affect the number of avalanche incidents in the backcountry. What's more, the correlation has grown stronger over the last 20 years.

I visited Moore in the fall of 2012 at his office in the Northwest Weather and Avalanche Center (NWAC). The 65-year-old is another legend in the snow science community who also—no big surprise—studied under Ed LaChapelle at the University of Washington. Moore led me through a maze of gray filing cabinets and flat-screen computer monitors to a cubicle where we could talk. He is a skier himself, a free spirit from the old days who still wears a gray ponytail and is known for rhyming forecasts. He retired from his post as the director of NWAC in 2012, after 37 years of service. The last forecast he wrote before he left: "So my wish is simple when the season is done. That no one has died, not even one."

Avalanche forecasting is highly dependent on weather forecasting, and after analyzing weather data between 1950 and 2012 and comparing it to avalanche incidents, Moore noticed a relationship. During La Niña years like 2011–2012, avalanche fatalities in the Northwest were slightly higher. During neutral or El Niño years, they were slightly lower.

Most skiers are familiar with La Niña and El Niño. They are technically Southern Oscillations in the Pacific Ocean that form when water in the eastern tropical Pacific is excessively warm (El Niño) or cool (La Niña). The resulting air-pressure differential affects Pacific weather patterns. In the U.S., El Niño years typically see a split Jet Stream, sending more precipitation and cooler weather across the southern tier of the U.S. and leaving the Northwest warmer and slightly drier. Conversely, during a La Niña year the Northwest is usually cooler and wetter and the south warmer and drier.

The average number of fatalities during an El Niño year in the Pacific Northwest is around 1.2. The average number during a La Niña year is more than twice that. If you look at the last 20 years, those numbers nearly double.[16] The difference between two and four deaths is hardly statistically significant, yet even accounting for more people in the backcountry the pattern is consistent—perhaps never more so than in 2011–2012. What's more, the trend is evident in varying degrees—sometimes in favor of La Niña, sometimes El Niño—throughout the West, and it will likely get worse as the planet warms.[17]

La Niña years in the Northwest typically see more distinct weather events, more precipitation, more loading and more chance for weak layers to develop and fail. In a word, Moore summarized, the snowpack becomes "unusual." And in 40 years of avalanche forecasting, abnormal conditions, he says, are typically what trip skiers up.

Several scientific papers—including the UNEP report Richard Armstrong contributed to—warn that climate change over the next 50 years will (1) significantly increase the likelihood of avalanches by changing the composition of the snowpack and (2) increase avalanche potency by depositing huge amounts of precipitation in the mountains at once. Another hazard the UNEP report points out: "Increasing events of rain-on-snow…may enhance the triggering of avalanche release. This is an increasing risk at lower elevations and in coastal mountains with rising winter temperatures."

To be clear, climate change didn't kill the men at Tunnel Creek. They died in an accident. Nothing more. But the conditions that set up the slide are similar to the ones forecasters are warning about for the future—winter rain events, longer periods between storms and extreme snowfall—and the avalanche serves as a wake-up call that as the atmosphere changes, the mountains are changing too. "You'd have more unusual conditions if you had the atmosphere warming by 6 degrees Celsius," Moore said. "You probably wouldn't be able to understand all of the things that were happening around you. I don't think people would handle it very well."

Something happens inside skiers' souls the moment they master their first turn, deflecting vectors that hold them down all day into ones that slingshot them forward. That seed keeps them coming back year after year, every stage of progress growing the obsession. The victims of the Tunnel Creek avalanche—John Brenan, Jim Jack and Chris Rudolph—were sustained by that passion. They represented the spirit of skiing so purely that their passing marked a kind of turning point in the sport. Perhaps like the months and years after Mark Foo died while surfing Mavericks, or when guides Rob Hall and Scott Fischer perished on Mount Everest.

The thrill that hooks a skier in the first place is the same one that lures him or her into near-vertical couloirs and down powder slopes layered in three feet of cold smoke. Those moments are pure living and, at times, can feel worth risking your life for. Flatlanders can call it irresponsible or absurd; it doesn't lessen the thrill. And it won't stop skiers. In the aftermath of Tunnel Creek, with the threat of climate change looming, that commitment may well be what the ski community needs to save its mountains and way of life.

As Dolores LaChapelle wrote, the skiing life means living close to the Earth. It means interacting with the forces that shaped our planet and understanding the cycles that maintain it. "I am not saying that skiing is necessarily a valid goal," she wrote, "but living is. Living in a particular place in a real relationship with the earth and the sky and the living beings around you—the fourfold of Heidegger—is a valid goal, as this relationship contributes to more being. Community is sharing a particular physical space, and environment, not only with other people but with the other beings of the place and fully realizing that the needs of all the beings of that place affect how you live your life. Such an awareness of relationships is a culture of awareness."

Chapter Eight
The Movement

The earth is flat and rides on air; in the same way the sun and the moon and the other heavenly bodies, which are all fiery, ride the air because of their flatness.

—*Anaximenes of Miletus*

T here was a time when the Earth was flat. Another when the sun and stars orbited our planet and the space between was the domain of angels and demons. These myths were not myths then. They were reality. Dragons lived beyond the edges of the oceans. Volcanoes and tornadoes moved at the will of the gods. The moon was a translucent orb.

Scientists have been admonished throughout history for contradicting theological explanations for the ways of the world. The idea of mankind discovering a scientific explanation for—much less controlling—the forces of nature is seen as arrogant and blasphemous by many. Even today it brings existential topics into play: spirituality, religion, the afterlife. The seed that we are mortals living at the whim of beings far larger than us was sown long ago. So when scientists began suggesting in the mid-20th century that humans were warming the Earth, the reaction was similar. Some people listened, but most dismissed the theories as preposterous. The reason, vice president of sustainability for Aspen Skiing Company

Auden Schendler says, is that it takes time for humans to change their perspective on long-held beliefs.

"Take Galileo as an example," he says. "Here's a guy who's such a smart dude, such a clear thinker, that he's able to say, even though it seems weird, 'My data says we've got to be moving around the sun.' If a sensible person like myself were around back then, I would think, 'You're an idiot. We'd feel the wind on our faces. And, by the way, the Earth is round, so we'd fall off the bottom.' Then his assistant says the moon's gravitational pull moves the tides. Galileo had this incredible commonsense view of the world. And he said, 'That's crazy. That can't be it.' He rejected that because it just seemed wacky."

Schendler has spent most of his adult life trying to convince people that climate science isn't wacky. He speaks often of the power of humanity— the power to create and to destroy. At Aspen Skiing Company his job is not to convince people to believe in something; rather, it's to advise senior management on energy efficiency, renewable-energy policy and generally how to navigate a warming world as a ski resort. He studied environmental science and biology at Bowdoin College and worked as a sustainable-business advisor at the Rocky Mountain Institute in Colorado before coming to Aspen in 2000. Since he arrived he has been a leading voice among an enlightened few in the fight to save snow.

"The challenge is that there's a big gap between what most people, and this includes the ski industry, think needs to happen and what actually needs to happen," he says. "The ski industry's response to climate change initially was, 'OK, let's reduce our carbon footprint.' And they said that because it makes sense from a business perspective, and it's good PR and what else can you do? The problem is that this is how most corporations and the ski industry are *still* responding. And it's not doing anything. This isn't climate strategy. The climate strategy is national policy of some sort; it's a national conversation, to change the whole economy of energy. There are many different ways that can happen, but it's not going to happen unless the politicians are forced to move. That's how it's always worked. As the famous quote from FDR talking to the labor guys went, 'I agree with you completely; now make me do it.'"

At first glance, Aspen is the last town where you'd expect to find the vanguard of ski resort sustainability. Roaring Fork Valley is the land of 50,000-square-foot houses, where celebrities like Ted Turner, Jimmy Buffett, George Lucas, Robert McNamara and Prince Bandar bin Sultan bin Abdulaziz of Saudi Arabia called home at one time. It's where Ivana Trump tussled with Marla Maples over Donald, where Kato Kaelin met Nicole Brown Simpson and where Claudine Longet shot ski sensation Spider Sabich, then married the attorney who represented her in the murder case.

Outside of town, though, there are real mountains, real people and real skiers. Aspen's main summit, Ajax, lurches straight up practically from downtown and the steep glades of Aspen Highlands and wide bowls of Snowmass are 15 minutes down the road. Well before the celebrities and gossip arrived, Dolores LaChapelle and Dick Durrance schussed these slopes. Around the same time, a visionary named Walter Paepcke initiated a campaign for national cultural reform—a concept he dubbed the "Aspen Idea" and that brought together intellectuals to discuss architecture, art, music and philosophy. Paepcke's idea eventually became the Aspen Institute, now an international nonprofit based in Washington, D.C., that has helped shape the progressive culture and international influence of the town.

As a new member of Aspen's illuminati, Schendler has never been afraid to speak his mind. The thesis of his book, *Getting Green Done: Hard Truths from the Front Lines of the Sustainability Revolution*, is that the time for symbolic steps to save the planet has passed. *Time* magazine recognized him in 2006 as a "global-warming innovator" and a slew of mainstream magazines have quoted and covered him. Though he works for a ski resort, his message and goals are far broader.

Schendler was a skier before he was an environmentalist. He didn't follow the same path that Jim Jack and Rob Castillo did, but he fell for the mountains with similar gusto. He was an Outward Bound instructor and Forest Service employee when he was younger and has climbed Alaska's Mount Denali and kayaked the Grand Canyon. He's been a skier since the 1980s—when, he says, "it was still cool to have a pair of skis on the roof of your car." Growing up in New Jersey, he skied Hunter Mountain and Sugarbush. "I remember being at the top of Sugarbush barely able to ski. K2 5500s, 205 centimeters. I remember thinking, 'How do you ski 400 Volkswagen-sized ice bumps?' And now that I'm a skier, I know that no one skis that."

Schendler has spent enough time in the mountains and around mountain people to know what alpine communities are capable of. So when he hears comments like Vail CEO Rob Katz's December 2012 op-ed in the *Denver Post*, which read, "When the effects of climate change really show up, no one will care about skiing at Aspen and Vail," he knows better. Most skiers have a college education. Many, especially in Aspen, are wealthy businesspeople who influence policymakers in Washington, D.C. So the fight to save snow, for Schendler, is actually a fight to get the ear of those who can effect more widespread change: senators, philanthropists, lobbyists.

"What has to happen is things like a national carbon tax or action by the EPA on existing power plants that's discussed and made national policy overtly by the president," he says. "We can't just do stealth emissions reductions. We have to talk about it so China and India can see that we're leading. The policy fix is not all that complicated. In one word, you have *deployment* of clean power technology, and to get there you have to change policy. And you have to make energy more expensive. You have to have standards for appliances and vehicles. You have to have incentives for clean energy; you have to have state and national energy standards. There needs to be some kind of pricing on carbon. That's what we're trying to use the ski industry to push."

The ski industry itself has been surprisingly slow to react to climate change, given that it could put the industry out of business. Ski resorts use a lot of energy. A single skier averages about 20 kilowatt-hours of energy consumption per day—the same amount a refrigerator uses in two weeks. Snowcats average six gallons of fuel an hour, and snowmaking is even more energy intensive. In 2009, before committing to a 10 percent reduction in consumption, Vail alone spent $27 million on energy.[18]

National Ski Area Association campaigns like "Keep Winter Cool" are moving in the right direction, but overall have done little to mitigate climate change. The NSAA first adopted a climate change policy in 2002, with a "reduce, educate, advocate" message. It has since encouraged ski areas to reduce greenhouse gases with initiatives and grants from the "Sustainable Slopes" and "Climate Challenge" programs.

But the truth is, with skier numbers relatively flat since 1979, most ski area executives spend their time keeping the business afloat—and have few resources left to lead the kind of nationwide push needed to force climate change legislation. Resort policies have varied from ignoring the problem completely to mocking it. In 2012 Vail Resorts ran an ad in *The New York Times* featuring skiers and snowboarders gliding through fresh powder under the headline, "The Climate HAS CHANGED." Katz then published his op-ed in the *Denver Post*, with the regrettable testimonial, "Count me in the category of someone who is very worried about climate change.... You can count me out of the group that says we need to address climate change to save skiing."

If the ski industry is to save itself—not to mention help save snow, alpine habitat and ecosystems downstream of the mountains—common sense says it will take a leadership role in decarbonizing the planet. Resorts like Jiminy Peak, which built a windmill to power its lifts, and the tiny Swiss resort of Tenna, whose double chair runs off of 82 solar panels strung above the lift, are leading the way but are in the minority. A popular strategy for many ski areas has been to purchase renewable energy certificates to "offset" a ski area's carbon footprint. What this means is the resort gives money to projects developing or producing renewable energy, to offset dirty energy a ski area uses. Resorts regularly claim to be "carbon neutral" after buying enough credits to offset their footprint. But the credits are often vastly underpriced, and not all offset money goes toward decarbonizing the planet. Though the programs can provide valuable funding for green projects, Schendler says, it's more of a Band-Aid in terms of greening the industry.

A 2008 study at Stanford looked at Kyoto–certified carbon offsets and found that nearly two-thirds were determined to be invalid for claiming initiatives like not clear-cutting a forest that a company wasn't going to cut anyway. In China and India recently more than a dozen factories were being compensated for capturing a coolant waste byproduct called HFC-23—that is 11,700 times more potent a greenhouse gas than carbon dioxide. Because they could get so much money for it, they started producing more of the waste to capture.[19]

Two years ago, Schendler proposed the kind of project he says is needed in the skiing world, not to mention the world at large. The nearby Elk Creek Mine was leaking methane into the atmosphere, as most coal mines do, and Schendler suggested working with a firm that could capture the gas and burn it in a generator to produce power for the resort. The resort financed the plan with $5.5 million, and the three-megawatt plant went online in 2012. It now generates 24 million kilowatt-hours of electricity annually—enough to power the entire Aspen Skiing Company and its four ski areas.

The plant will pay off at 12 percent and break even in seven years, Schendler says. Aspen already has plans to build a second one. Because the project destroys methane in the process, it is carbon negative, saving the same amount of annual carbon dioxide emissions as a 600-megawatt solar plant.

The project isn't without critics. Even though the mine has existed for a decade, environmentalists say the proper solution is to shut it down—not give it a reason to continue digging six million tons of coal every year. To complicate the matter further, the mine's owner is oil baron and billionaire Bill Koch. In an *Aspen Business Journal* article, Elk Creek Mine president Jim Cooper summed up the attitude that much of the American business world has adopted toward climate change: "We put a lot of money into it, and I told Bill Koch this, 'If Oxbow Mining doesn't get anything but some PR out of this, it may be worth it to me.' We took something that has very negative public views to it and now it's something that's useable.…I really do not believe in manmade climate change because I believe man is giving himself too damn much credit. I'm thankful every morning that I walk out on my porch in Paonia that I'm not faced with a saber-toothed tiger."

Environmentalists have battled this kind of old-boy mentality for ages.

"Live and let live" is a time-honored ethos in America. It's a worthy code when dealing with neighbors, lawyers and anyone with a gun. The twist that climate change brings to the mix is that doing nothing makes it worse. The greatest challenge global warming presents, Schendler says, is one that Americans might not be ready for.

"Climate change doesn't make any sense to people," he says. "It's too obscure, too big, too surprising that we can have such an impact. The narrative of our story is very complimentary. We're not fools. Every single thing that made Americans great is this commonsensical approach. We needed to defeat Hitler. It was going to hurt. Let's do it. But that gut-level common sense that made America great becomes a liability when dealing with climate change."

Back in the primordial epoch of skinny skis, a young snowboarder pioneered the mountains of the West, shaping a style and career that would change snowboarding, and skiing, forever. Jeremy Jones grew up on Cape Cod and ski raced in Vermont as a kid. He took his first snowboard run on a Cape Cod golf course in 1982 and had to ride his board out-of-bounds on family ski trips to Stowe because the resort boycotted snowboards at the time. When they dropped the ban, Jones was the first rider to be "certified" to ride there.

Jones started competing when he was 14 and couch-surfed his way to more than 30 contests every winter—powered by hundreds of peanut-butter-and-jelly sandwiches. He was 16 when he visited his older brothers, Todd and Steve, who were living in Jackson Hole, Wyoming, and decided to dedicate the rest of his life to riding the highest, steepest peaks in the world. While Todd and Steve went on to build a film-production empire with Teton Gravity Research, Jeremy spent more time in what had become his favorite playground: Alaska. He snowboarded more first descents—and what can only be described as "unthinkable" descents—than can be listed and soon stood alongside snowboarding legends like Jim Zellers and Craig Kelly. *Snowboarder* magazine voted him Big Mountain Rider of the Year 10 years in a row, and in 2013 National Geographic honored him as one of its Adventurers of the Year, alongside space-B.A.S.E. jumper Felix Baumgartner.

Jones is an introspective, soft-spoken soul who felt at home in the backcountry from an early age. He built his first splitboard—a snowboard that separates into two touring skis—by sawing one in half and used it to climb into the peaks. He was hiking just such a peak in Fernie, British Columbia, in 2006 when the local he was climbing with mentioned that a few years ago they would have been able to snowboard right where they were. But since the temperature and the snowline had climbed higher, they had to keep hiking.

It takes a focused, unwavering mind to stare down a 55-degree face on a snowboard. It takes a similar mindset to take on an environmental cause many people either don't believe in or are unaware of. Jones read up on climate change and saw its effects in other mountains he traveled to. He formed an advocacy group called Protect Our Winters in 2007 and brought TGR's marketing director, Chris Steinkamp, onboard as executive director. The initiative started off like most environmental efforts do: with a website and some PR. But POW was different from other startups. Within an hour of the site being finished, donations started flowing in.

"It was kind of proof that there was this gap between the effect that climate change was having on our sport and the action being taken by us to address it," Steinkamp says. "What was actually being done was nothing. And so that's why we started this. The whole idea of Protect Our Winters from the beginning was to unify the winter-sports community. We could get 21 million people who ride and ski in the U.S. and start mobilizing them right away."

Steinkamp is a lifelong skier himself. He grew up in New York's Westchester County and learned to ski at a ma-and-pa hill near Brewster. From there he graduated to Stowe, then St. Lawrence University and nearby Whiteface Mountain. Then, finally, Aspen, where he fell in love with the Rockies, the West and skiing powder.

Jones and Steinkamp are unlikely heroes in the world of environ-mental activism. Jones began his career flying to snow-capped peaks in helicopters, and Steinkamp cut his teeth as an ad executive in Los Angeles, working for the car industry. What Steinkamp learned in the trenches of national car campaigns, though, was incredibly relevant to spreading the word about climate change.

"It's surprising how similar the two are," he says. "We're trying to mobilize a community; we're trying to create a brand. Protect Our Winters is not a normal nonprofit, and it really helps to be a marketing guy in this situation. Before, I was trying to get people to buy a car, and now I'm trying to get people to vote the right way."

As the window closes to keep warming to a reasonable level, Steinkamp says, there's only one choice left: "We have to literally to start forcing our economic weight in Washington." The idea changed the course of POW's mission and originated with none other than Schendler, who joined the group's board of directors in 2010. In 2012, POW and the Natural Resources Defense Council published a report that put the threat of warming winters in a vocabulary regular Americans, and Washington, could understand: dollars and cents. Two University of New Hampshire researchers, Elizabeth Burakowski and Matthew Magnusson, compiled the paper. Both are Ph.D. candidates in the University of New Hampshire's interdisciplinary Natural Resources and Earth Systems Science program.

"Climate Impacts on the Winter Tourism Economy in the United States" was published in December 2012 and was immediately broadcast on mainstream news outlets across the country. The statistic that grabbed readers' attention wasn't just that snow was disappearing, but that low snowfall over the last 10 years had cost the winter tourism industry $1 billion and 27,000 jobs.

The report goes on to break down winter tourism income and jobs across the country, including past effects, both direct and indirect, and future projections. The fact that state and local governments took in $1.4 billion in taxes from winter tourism in 2009–2010, while the federal government received $1.7 billion, made it clear that the snow business was an economic engine. By the report's conclusion, it becomes apparent that the industry is teetering on the edge of an uncertain future, with a surprisingly large sector of the U.S. economy at stake:

> Surmised from all this data is a portrait of the American winter landscape with more than three-quarters of states benefitting economically from these winter sports and 211,900 jobs either directly or indirectly supported by the industry. The ramifications of changing snow fall patterns are already altering people's outdoor habits—taking an economic toll on the ski resort industry of over $1 billion in the last decade. Without intervention, winter temperatures are projected to warm an additional 4 to 10 degrees Fahrenheit by the end of the century, with subsequent decreases in snow cover area, snowfall, and shorter snow season. Snow depths could decline in the west by 25 to 100 percent. The length of the snow season in the northeast will be cut in half. In order to protect winter—and the hundreds of thousands whose livelihoods depend upon a snow-filled season—we must act now to support policies that protect our climate, and in turn, our slopes.

The report hit its mark in Washington and POW has kept the pressure on since. On April 11, 2013, Jones was recognized as a "Champion of Change" at the White House, part of President Obama's "Winning the Future" initiative. POW followed up with a hand-delivered letter signed by 75 winter-sports athletes advocating climate change legislation. Some of the athletes who signed it were on their way home from training in Sochi, Russia, for the 2014 Winter Olympics—where two events in February 2013 were cancelled due to lack of snow. Sochi organizers stored snow collected the rest of that year to use in 2014, in case there wasn't enough.

If POW's idea was to nudge Washington closer to climate change legislation, it worked. In June 2013, President Obama announced an extensive and long-awaited "Climate Action Plan." The authority by which the president will execute the plan hinges on a lawsuit the Aspen Skiing Company helped bring attention to in 2007. Even more relevant to the skiing community, Obama cited in his speech the Climate Declaration that 108 ski resorts and other businesses signed in the spring of 2013—and which Schendler flew to Washington to release. "Mountain communities worry about what smaller snowpacks will mean for tourism," the president said, "and then, families at the bottom of the mountains wonder what it will mean for their drinking water."

Some of the most winter-tourism-dependent states—like Wyoming, Montana and Utah—also happen to be major producers of coal, oil and natural gas. So they are dead against emissions limits. The paradox is emblematic of the impasse that has held up climate change legislation around the world. Governments, manufacturers and energy companies are hesitant to shut off the carbon pipeline as they try to avoid financial meltdown—the problem being that the longer they wait, the worse the consequences will be.

Most scientists agree that 2 degrees Celsius (3.6 degrees Fahrenheit)—the U.N.-mandated climate change limit—is the tipping point between climate change humans can adapt to and something that would result in global chaos. With less than 2 degrees Celsius of warming, we will still have snow, food and water availability and a habitable climate in most regions. Higher than 2 degrees Celsius, most analysts predict economic, financial and even societal collapse in many parts of the world.[20]

The American Meteorological Society suggested in a study that we are headed in that direction, predicting a 90 percent chance of 3.5 to 7.4 degrees Celsius of warming by 2100. Even conservative entities like the World Bank, PricewaterhouseCoopers and the International Energy Agency are now advising their clients to forget about 2 degrees Celsius and prepare for a planet 4 to 6 degrees Celsius warmer. In a report in 2012, PricewaterhouseCoopers stated,

> It's time to plan for a warmer world....We have passed a critical threshold – not once since World War 2 has the world achieved that rate of decarbonisation, but the task now confronting us

is to achieve it for 39 consecutive years....Even doubling our current rate of decarbonisation, would still lead to emissions consistent with 6 degrees of warming by the end of the century. To give ourselves a more than 50% chance of avoiding 2 degrees will require a six-fold improvement in our rate of decarbonisation.

A recent paper from the Global Carbon Project reported on the growing "inertia" of climate change, due to the failure of "carbon sinks"—like the ability of the ocean to dissolve carbon dioxide—and potential feedbacks like a dieback of the Amazon forest, which could amplify warming by 5 to 30 percent over the next century. Carbon dioxide emissions from fossil fuels increased by 41 percent between 1990 and 2008, 1990 being the benchmark that countries at the Kyoto Protocol committed to scale emissions back to.[21]

Predictions of life on Earth with 4 degrees Celsius of warming are grim, including life-threatening heat waves, declining global food supply and a sudden rise in the sea level of 10 feet or more. The report *Turn Down the Heat*, commissioned by the World Bank in 2012, predicted that coral reefs will begin to dissolve, midsummer temperatures in parts of the Middle East will approach 113 degrees Fahrenheit, drought-affected cropland could rise from 15 percent today to 44 percent and water availability will drop drastically as watersheds like the Ganges basin dry up.[22]

As for a 6 degrees Celsius change, writer Mark Lynas summed it up in 2007 after researching reports on the subject, speculating that it "would catapult the planet into an extreme greenhouse state not seen for nearly 100 million years, when dinosaurs grazed on polar rainforests and deserts reached into the heart of Europe. It would cause a mass extinction of almost all life and probably reduce humanity to a few struggling groups of embattled survivors clinging to life near the poles."

Speculation aside, the message is clear, Schendler says. The snowball is growing and nearly every aspect of life on Earth is at risk. "The big fear is that you basically bankrupt our country, or our world, to the point that it becomes a survival society—versus doing anything that makes human society advance and makes us happy," he says. "You lose everything you care about and all you're doing is rebuilding bridges and building seawalls. It's sort of what Osama bin Laden was trying to do to the U.S.—make us focus on war and bankrupt us so we don't spend money on schools.... Who cares if you can't go ski? Skiing and art and music and culture, all of these 'disposable things' are what make human societies flourish and are what moves us forward. What if we lose that? Well, that would be a greater tragedy than anything else."

Chapter Nine
On the Road

Then said Jesus unto him, Except you see signs and wonders, you will not believe.

—*John 4:48*

Humans must see to believe. It's in our nature, part of the complex epistemological process that determines what we *know*, When it's hot outside, pollsters find that more people believe in climate change. When it's cold, more think climate change is a hoax. According to a 2013 study in the journal *Climatic Change*, a 1 degree Celsius temperature increase equates to a 10 percent increase in the percentage of people worried about global warming.[23] In an AP-GfK poll in 2009, 47 percent of Americans "with little or no trust in scientists" believed the world was getting warmer. In 2012, 61 percent believed in climate change.

Most attribute the uptick in believers to the extreme weather of 2012. There were 34,000 daily high-temperature records set in 2012, with almost 100 million people experiencing 10 or more 100-degree days. Flooding, drought and wildfires across South America, Australia and Africa and "super typhoons" in the Western Pacific and China made headlines as well. In the U.S., the warm and dry climate led to more than nine million acres burning in the West.

In the fall of 2012, Hurricane Sandy eclipsed even Hurricane Katrina in size and damage, spanning 1,000 miles of the East Coast and cutting off power to eight million households. By then, heat waves across the Lower 48, and low snowpack from the previous winter, had left 63 percent of the continental U.S. consumed by drought—and more than half of the counties in America designated as disaster areas. By the end of the year, the U.S. had suffered 11 natural disasters that cost $1 billion or more. An economist at Deutsche Bank Securities suggested the expense would drop the U.S. GDP by an entire percentage point.

It's a dangerous game to chalk up a single year, much less a single storm, to climate change. But to skeptics, and a few scientists, 2012 was the proof they needed. James Hansen—a distinguished NASA scientist who retired in April 2013 to fight global warming—published an op-ed in the *Washington Post* in August 2012 that stated, "For the extreme hot weather of the recent past, there is virtually no explanation other than climate change." Other reports suggested that massive droughts were more than 20 times more likely to occur now than in the 1960s, and that sea levels were rising 60 percent faster than previously thought. In February 2013 a study by Duke University found that still only half of all Americans were "convinced" the climate was changing.[24]

That same month, I set out on a 1,000-mile road trip to see for myself what was going on in the Western U.S. After reading about climate change for months, and watching senators, environmentalists and lobbyists debate it endlessly, I wanted to talk to people who actually lived in the snow—ski bums, patrollers, avalanche forecasters, ranchers—about what *they* were seeing. So I packed my skis and headed out West, hoping to find answers at Mount Hood, Stevens Pass, Big Sky and Jackson Hole—and bird-dog a few powder stashes along the way.

Flying into Portland, Oregon, the first day of the trip, a haze hung over the foothills surrounding the city. It looked warm down there, not like mid-February. In the old days, snowfall in Portland wasn't uncommon. In 1950 the city got 41 inches of snow in January alone. Now it looked like a spring day. "Ninety miles from Portland," the captain said. "Clear skies, 56 degrees, winds out of the west at 10 miles per hour."

The next day, I woke to low, gunmetal-gray clouds pushing down on the city. I made my way past the crab shacks, tropical-green bike lanes and red-light sex shops downtown, east to a National Weather Service facility near the shores of the Columbia River. The building looked like a one-story mini-mall, with blinds pulled over the windows and Toyota pickup trucks and compact sedans lined up in the parking lot. NWS meteorologist Jeremiah Pyle met me at the door and led me through a labyrinth of computer monitors displaying images of what the weather was doing, had done and might do over the next 72 hours.

Most meteorologists focus on short-range forecasts, and none that I met on the trip was interested in speculating too far into the future. Pyle did say he looked at things he called "teleconnections," like the Madden-Julian Oscillation near Indonesia that can send moisture to the Pacific Northwest. Most big snowstorms in the Cascades, he said, occur when a moisture plume from the tropics meets a storm track somewhere around the Gulf of Alaska, then continues to the coast. When Pyle sees those events line up, he loads his skis into the car so he can head to the mountains after work.

The Cascades mark the border between a mild, maritime climate in the west and a sunnier, drier continental climate to the east. Winter in much of western Oregon and Washington hovers precariously close to the freezing level, making the region particularly vulnerable to climate change. Temperatures have risen around 1.5 degrees Fahrenheit since 1920 and the area has lost 25 percent of its snowpack. Conservative estimates suggest the temperature will climb more than 5 degrees Fahrenheit by 2080, leaving the entire region with 40 to 70 percent less snow.[25]

Pyle hasn't seen much change in the high alpine, he said, where snowfall has remained fairly consistent. The biggest changes he's seen are at lower elevations, like a 30 percent decrease in snow accumulation at an NWS study plot on Mount Hood. The plot is set 5,000 feet above sea level, near the town of Government Camp. "Between 1950 to 1970, an average of 300 inches of snow used to fall there," he said. "Since 1975 it has dropped to 225 inches."

There was no snow in sight when I left the forecasting center and followed Highway 84 along the Columbia River. It was Wednesday and traffic was light as I turned south onto the Mount Hood Highway and cruised past fast-food joints and sprawling box stores. There were rose gardens and small vineyards on the other side of the road, and rows of cabbage and lettuce that looked ready to be picked.

It started to rain as the road bowed east around Sandy River, tall pines crowding the two-lane highway. The classic old ski hotels and greasy-spoon restaurants you find at the periphery of ski resorts edged the streets of Mount Hood Village. I passed the Snowline Lodge, with its signature Northwestern drive-through espresso stand, and noted that the building was probably situated close to the snowline when it was constructed. For more than a century that line has been moving up, inch by inch, marching its way toward the great white skirts of 11,239-foot Mount Hood itself.

The science and magic of snowfall played out as I gained altitude, passing through a rainforest down low then entering a land of snow and ice up high. All it took was a few degrees of cooling for the gloomy gray to morph into brilliant white, the most beautiful white coming down outside Valian's Ski Shop in Government Camp, where Bud Valian has been tuning skis since 1968.

Valian learned to ski in British Columbia in 1947—on wooden boards with wire coat hangers to hold the toes of his ski boots in place. The 80-year-old moved to Mount Hood in 1954 to teach skiing at Timberline. Timberline Lodge was quite a scene back then. Constructed between 1936 and 1938 by workers from FDR's Works Progress Administration, it became the hippest winter resort in the Cascades when the Magic Mile chairlift opened in 1939. Thanks to epic snowfall, and the Palmer Glacier, today it is the only ski area in the States that offers skiing every month of the year—making it a destination for ski teams, ski testers and camps of all sorts during the summer.

Back in the day, Valian used to snowshoe to the top of the Magic Mile, shovel off the exit ramp and ski back to the lodge for breakfast before starting his day. He remembers there weren't any stop signs or streetlights in town, and that there were more restaurants and businesses. He also recalls that there used to be more snow. "Even though we've had lean years, and some real horrendous snow years," he said, "the one thing I do know is that the average elevation of the snowline is 1,200 to 1,400 feet higher now than it was back then."

It is hard to gaze at the heap of ice and rock that is Mount Hood and conclude that the mountain is in need of a good blizzard. The peak looks like a scoop of ice cream melting into the deep-green forest of north-western Oregon. Its flanks swoop up from old-growth fir and hemlock and meet the mountain's prominent ridges—Cooper Spur, Yocum and Lang—which, in turn, extend like shadowy arms to the summit. Hood is a stratovolcano, a solitary blip on the Columbia Gorge's vertical profile, with no major mountains within 40 miles to steal its thunder. As for snow, every winter it is buried under more than 35 feet of the stuff.

Yet several of the mountain's 12 glaciers have receded up to 60 percent since the early 1900s and climatologists are predicting a slow upward creep of the snowline and shorter winter seasons across the Northwest. Studies have already found that springtime snowpack in parts of the region has dropped from 50 to 75 percent—more than anywhere else in the country.[26] By mid-century, it's likely that it will disappear completely in the summer—bad news for the summer ski camps on Mount Hood that see 1,000 kids every day.

That night I drove a few miles to Mount Hood Skibowl to get some runs in. The resort was founded in 1928 and is one of the oldest operating ski areas in the States. It's the largest night-skiing resort in the country and had the empty beer cans and cigarette butts on-slope to prove it. It was snowing hard by the time I saw the lights of Skibowl glowing in the night. A small crowd of teenagers sat around a bonfire at the base, and a lonely bartender wandered around the lodge, listening to the radio.

The lift was eerily empty, and as I rode up, each descending chair emerged from the mist like a ghost. At the top I peeled off onto Lower Bowl. I couldn't see the run well under the dim lights, but I could feel gravity pulling me downhill. After all of the flying, interviewing and driving, the sensation of skiing even an intermediate groomer was sublime. The trail was edged with giant hemlock coated in thick, wet snow. I didn't make a turn the whole way down, just followed the contours of the mountain and trail until I could see the bonfire, rosy-cheeked teenagers and silhouette of the base lodge at the bottom.

The next morning the NWS forecast read, "20 percent chance of snow before 10am. Mostly cloudy, with a high near 36F." Outside, it was cold and gray with a kind of snow-hail coming down that I'd never seen before. I watched the climate change as I drove down Highway 35, gliding over Hood's glacial moraines, rockslides and streams to Hood River Valley. There, skeletal apple and pear trees reached back from the road in perfect rows. Back in the day, fruit trees were about the only crop you could find on the valley floor. As the Northwest warmed over the last 30 years, though, the area started growing grapes that once made Napa Valley famous—600 miles to the south.

I pulled into one of the vineyards and spoke with farmer Steve Bickford. Bickford grew up in the house adjacent to the parking lot, and his son-in-law, John Stehlik, now runs the business. The state recently named Bickford Orchards a Century Farm, meaning the Bickfords had been farming in the valley for more than 100 years. Stehlik showed us the farm's bottling machine and casks of pinot gris and Riesling stacked up in the warehouse. In 2012 the farm put out 30,000 bottles of wine.

Like many other farmers in the region, the Bickfords transitioned into the wine business a decade ago after a shortage of water, inconsistent weather and market changes made some of the farm's pear and apple orchards unviable. Wine grapes don't need as consistent a water supply and thrive in the warm summers and shoulder seasons that the valley has seen over the last decade. The warmer it gets, the better the grapes grow, Stehlik said. And the warmer it gets everywhere else—like Napa Valley, Bickford added—the more demand there is for grapes in northern regions like Oregon and Washington.

Down the road, I passed the gourmet sandwich shops and kite-surfing stores of Hood River then followed Route 84 past The Dalles hydro-electric dam—where in 2006 Google built its first rural data center to take advantage of cheap, sustainable power. The move encouraged nearby

Biglow Canyon Wind Farm to expand and spurred the creation of the nation's first renewable-energy training program. I weaved through the monolithic spinning turbines up Highway 97 to the edge of the Columbia Plateau. The landscape there was flat all the way to the horizon, with only sagebrush growing in the rusty brown soil. A few dirt roads and dried-up arroyos crisscrossed the landscape—sectioned off by barbed wire fences and solitary telephone poles every 100 yards. In the distance, I could see the white heap of 12,280-foot Mount Adams.

Driving through such varied landscapes hour after hour—high alpine to river valley to volcanic plateau to conifer forest—it hit me that there is a reason why the desert is a desert and farmland is farmland. And that it hasn't always been that way. Fifteen million years ago massive basaltic lava flows and the greatest floods in geological history shaped eastern Washington. The resulting contours of the mountains and prairies, in turn, now determine where rain falls and where it flows. It's not luck or evil spirits or divine intervention that makes a landscape fertile, barren, snowy or flooded. It's the evolution of the Earth itself.

I followed Highway 97 to Yakima and Ellensburg, then cut through the Wenatchee National Forest to Blewett Pass—on the old Yellowstone Trail—on the way to Leavenworth and Stevens Pass. The entire Northwest got hammered early in the 2012–2013 winter, with 3 to 5 feet of snow falling during Thanksgiving week, then 10 feet in December. January and the first half of February were largely dry, except for a few storms, then the snow started again and didn't stop until April.

It was another great season for Stevens—which logged more than 500 inches of snow—considering that much of the rest of the country had spotty conditions once again. The Sierra got deep early snow, then hardly anything in January and February. Colorado missed all of the early storms, and many resorts were half open for the Christmas holiday. On January 22 Aspen had a 22-inch base, but the snow picked up soon after that and a flush February and March pushed snow depths closer to average. The big winners were the Pacific Northwest, Northern Rockies and, surprisingly, the East Coast, which saw good snow almost all season long.

Apart from the hundreds of millions of dollars that the oil industry invests in anti-global-warming press, one of the reasons people have such a hard time believing in climate change is that it doesn't happen uniformly. Skeptics often claim that the planet hasn't warmed since 1998. That year happened to be exceptionally warm, and nine of the warmest years in recorded history have occurred since then. Global warming comes in step changes over a long period of time. So a region can see terrific back-to-back winters while, overall, warming accelerates and total snowpack declines. Another anomaly is that warmer air holds more moisture, so while there will be fewer winter storms in the future, the ones that hit the U.S. will bring more snow. Case in point: the number of extreme snowstorms in the U.S. has doubled since 1963, but total snowpack is down.[27]

When I woke up the next day, the sky was so blue it looked like one of the Bavarian murals in Leavenworth. The canyon was still dark, though, as I worked my way up to Stevens Pass. The previous fall, Mark Moore explained a phenomenon that makes low passes like Stevens skiable. Cold, high-pressure air from eastern Washington flows west through the passes when low-pressure storm fronts track east—freezing Cascadian summits and allowing precipitation to fall as snow instead of rain. "You really have to be aware of what the vertical profile of the atmosphere is in the mountains here," he said. "Stevens and Snoqualmie would not be the areas they are except for the easterly flow. They would get a lot more rain, especially should we slowly warm up."

Stevens looked stacked with powder when I arrived to ski with Tiffany Abraham. She met me at the fire pit outside the base lodge where Jack, Rudolph, Castillo and the Tunnel Creek crew gathered almost exactly a year before. I wasn't in town to talk about the accident this time, and Tiffany and I were both relieved to simply ski during her "riding hour." She'd gotten a job as group-sales coordinator for the resort and was allowed to ski for an hour on the clock. She was still deep in the ups and downs of grieving, she said. The only thing that made her feel better on a bad day was to put on her skis and get up on the mountain.

We did just that on the SkyLine Express chairlift, where she pointed out Big Chief and Cowboy Mountain—then mentioned, almost as an afterthought, that Tunnel Creek was on the backside. It hadn't snowed in weeks, but by the plumes of powder chasing Tiffany on our first run, you wouldn't know it. The sun was hot on the next lift ride up and Tiffany said she couldn't remember a time when there were so many sunny days on the pass. At the bottom of the next run we skied through dripping trees and slushy moguls, and Abraham said she had to go back to work.

We met up after the lifts closed at The Bull's Tooth for an après drink. Tiffany told me about the memorial they were planning for Jack, Brenan and Rudolph a few days from then. There was going to be an "adult-themed" scavenger hunt, and family and friends were dressing up in costumes. At the top of the Tunnel Creek drainage, near a wooden ski carved with the men's names, they planned to spread ashes and flowers.

The shock and heartache of the avalanche were clearly still with her, as was the kind of indomitable strength she seems to have exhibited most of her life. We ordered a round of shots of her favorite new drink, Ullr schnapps, and made a toast to the future. After tipping them back, I read the prayer printed on the side of the bottle:

Prayer for Snow

Come snow! Come snow!
Fall fast, fall slow
Be it powder or crud,
Let the inches be shown

Come snow! Come snow!
Blessed Ullr bestow
Make white our peaks
Make full our bowls

Come snow! Come snow!
From here to fro
Let the snow god be praised
Let his gifts be shown

The ridges of Stevens Pass were hidden behind a white mist in the morning. I had 600 miles to cover to get to Bozeman, Montana, and a day to do it in. So I got going early and made my way south along the Columbia River to I-90. There were orchards and vineyards along the way. In Wenatchee I drove by the college where Jim Jack, Murray Wais and Steve Winter started their careers, then past the road to Mission Ridge Ski Resort.

Hours later, near the border with Idaho, a long line of clouds moved in from the south. They ran west–east and I sped up to get ahead of them. There were snow showers in the forecast; a Pacific front was barreling from the coast toward Montana. I wanted to get there first and ski fresh powder the next day. I drove straight until 10:00 p.m., then stopped at the Broken Arrow Steak House in Deer Lodge. I'd been driving for nine hours straight and ordered a steak dinner, baked potato, apple pie and a coffee. Cowboys in 10-gallon hats sat around long tables, chewing on prime rib and talking about livestock and the weather. The place had been taking in travelers for almost 50 years, so when the waitress saw me relax a bit too long she asked, "You looked outside?" I told her no. "I ain't never seen wind and snow like that," she said, shaking her head.

She poured my coffee into a to-go cup and I headed out the door, where the storm had caught up and was blowing snow sideways. The car rocked from side to side through the valley as I pushed toward Homestake Pass. A bright flashing sign announced a detour on I-90 due to high winds on the pass. A big storm meant a big powder day, so I went for it anyway. There are swirling strobe lights on all of the big passes in Montana, and the green and white beams sliced through the dark as I crested the breach. The glowing Our Lady of the Rockies statue shone atop the Continental Divide above Butte and dozens of mining-head frames, illuminated by red lights, blazed in town.

The mountains held the storm up long enough for me to get in front of it, and I dropped down into the next valley. The forest was black and I spotted the Big Dipper overhead. An hour and a half later, I rolled into Bozeman.

The next morning I met up with a man who knows snow as well as anyone in Montana. Doug Chabot is the director of the Gallatin National Forest Avalanche Center. He moved to Montana 26 years ago and ski patrolled at Bridger Bowl before starting at the center. He is an avid skier and climber who spent the fall of 2011 putting routes up unclimbed peaks in northern Pakistan. All in all he's spent 24 years in the snow business in Montana.

Chabot and two full-time forecasters spend each morning interpreting weather models from the NWS, University of Utah and Unisys before fine-tuning them for the mountains around Bozeman. What skiers around Big Sky's Lone Peak, an hour southwest, look for is a strong southwest or western flow to bring snow, Chabot said. Bridger Bowl, located a half hour northeast, does better in a northwestern flow—or in something locals call the "Bridger Bowl cloud." "They can get four to six inches an hour in the cloud; it's insane how much snow falls," he said.

The Northern Rockies sit at the intersection of several storm flows and typically do well with snow. El Niño and La Niña are not as influential here, and the snowpack is what avalanche experts call "intermountain"—more stable than the shallow continental snowpack farther south in Colorado. Even though snow totals up high have been consistent, Chabot says, things are changing.

"I've definitely noticed a shift," he said. "Rain events in the middle of the winter used to be rare. In the last eight years or so, it seems we're getting them at least once a year, if not multiple times. And it's not just at the lower elevations. We'll have rain events up to 8,000 to 9,000 feet. It's just so bizarre in January or February to be talking about rain."

Chabot doesn't foresee the end of snow or skiing, but he does see big changes in what kind of snow falls and when. Shorter seasons and no snow at lower elevations are in store. Harkening back to Armstrong and Moore's warnings, he also said that rain events, in addition to other effects of climate change, are increasing avalanche danger in the region. He has recorded warmer temperatures earlier in the season—a situation that leads to wet avalanches in March instead of April. One of the most incredible things he's witnessed as Montana heats up: a gradual trans-formation across the state from an intermountain snowpack toward a continental one.

"The storms are acting what I call 'more bipolar,' too," he said. "We get these crazy swings. We might get a big snowstorm that feels like winter, followed by unseasonably warm, sometimes record-breaking temperatures. They have this manic feeling to them. We can't just settle into winter anymore."

Bob Dixon has worked and skied at Big Sky for more than 30 years and has seen much of what Chabot pointed out. He's been the ski patrol director for most of that time and has perhaps the most marvelous hair in the sport—shaped into a perfect sandy-brown coif from a lifetime of skiing *sans chapeau*. He agreed that snow at Big Sky is wetter in the early season and said that he has seen more rain events in the winter—like four years ago, when it rained to the summit six times in the first two months of the season. Overall, he said, the thermometer is rising.

"The first year I was here, in 1974, we had a cold snap where the still-air temperature got down to 62 below," he said. "And that was for six or seven days. That's when I learned to heat the oil pan underneath my car to warm up the engine enough to start it. We've seen a couple days at 20 or 30 below this winter, but nothing continuous."

It was still snowing that morning as I drove past old homesteader cabins along the Gallatin River to ride the largest ski area in the U.S. I could see neighboring Moonlight Basin and the posh, private Yellowstone Club from the Lone Peak Tram. The snow report said the storm had dumped nine inches on Big Sky, but the snow was over my knees 15 minutes later when I dropped into Otter Slide and skied it to Marx.

The secret to finding powder at Big Sky is knowing where the wind blows it. It apparently blew most of the summit snow into The Gullies, where I skied the next run in tracked powder. Near the end of the second gully I arced right into a white apron of fluff, and for the first time on the trip my skis lifted up in the new snow and I didn't touch bottom. I subtly shifted my weight from right to left as I floated through the cold smoke. By the bottom of the run, I had ice caked to my five-day-old stubble and around my goggles. Riding up the lift a few minutes later, I spotted my tracks—a deep, shadowy trench wending around the rocks.

Climatologists like to talk about cycles. The carbon cycle, the heat cycle. The water cycle was easy to recognize on the drive from Bozeman to Jackson Hole, Wyoming. Through Four Corners and toward Ennis on Highway 84, snow covered the high peaks and draped over ridgelines and draws all the way down to the ranchland of southwestern Montana. South of Black's Ford, water rushed through the Madison River, where, 20 feet from shore, I saw a fly-fisherman wearing a winter hat. Farther south, in Island Park, an enormous reservoir captured water and channeled it into potato- and soy-field irrigation ditches, and farther south still, at a hydroelectric dam in Palisades, outflowing water from the Snake River turned four 44-megawatt turbines.

The night before, I'd spoken to rancher Allen Carter near Livingston. Carter's family homesteaded Paradise Valley in the 1800s after bringing a wagon train north from Texas. On his grandmother's journey, she camped on the same field where Custer made his famous last stand—among teepee rings and debris left over from the battle. Carter and local ranchers had a "snow guy" who wandered the mountains in the spring and told them how much snowmelt they could expect. Though he didn't believe that humans were causing climate change, he said snowmelt had gone down recently. This year the mini-hydro plant his family runs on Pine Creek had to go offline three months early because of lack of runoff.

As I approached Jackson Hole and the end of the road trip, it struck me how many people I spoke with had little idea of what *might* happen to winter—and the planet. Whether they believed in anthropogenic climate change or not, it was surprising that not even snow experts I spoke with realized just how hot scientists are saying it might get. When I mentioned a 4 to 6 degrees Celsius spike in global temperature, most skiers, patrollers, meteorologists and ranchers sat back in disbelief and answered something like, "Well, if *that's* the case...," then revised their outlook on winter on a warming planet.

If an asteroid came dangerously close to Earth, as DA14 did in 2012, there are few who would question the science of the asteroid's trajectory. The fact that it *might* hit Earth is enough. Climate change is different in many ways, but the threat is similar: a drastic change to the composition of the atmosphere, climate, weather and life on Earth. Every snow expert I spoke with agreed that the planet was warming, and that they could see it in their daily lives. And yet many whose livelihoods depended on snow were noncommittal about what might be causing it—despite the fact that nearly every scientist studying the issue, in addition to several Forbes 500 companies and the Department of Defense, agrees that humans are warming the planet.

According to the 2004 Millennium Ecosystem Assessment, a report from 1,360 scientists that the U.N. commissioned to assess the state of the global environment, 16 of the 25 natural systems that humans need for survival are currently being used unsustainably: "At the heart of this assessment is a stark warning," the report reads. "Human activity is putting such strain on the natural functions of Earth that the ability of the planet's ecosystems to sustain future generations can no longer be taken for granted."[28] The Global Footprint Network found similar results in 2009, calculating that we passed Earth's ability to sustainably support humanity around 1986. The current human population requires 140 percent of available land to survive.

At the Montana-Idaho state line near Henry's Lake, global warming seemed like an abstract concept. Snowdrifts on the side of the road were 15 feet tall and a few flakes swooped over the windshield of the car. A low-pressure trough 15 vertical miles overhead was pushing another storm system east, and it was supposed to snow from Bozeman to Jackson all week. Eight snowmobiles lined up at a gas station when I pulled in to get coffee, and the blizzard began in earnest. The road was slick farther south and I slowed beneath the sheer peaks of Targhee National Forest.

Beyond Victor and Driggs, I climbed Teton Pass and saw ski tracks in the open meadows near the top, then a pair of skiers stepping over a snowbank. It had been snowing like hell for most of the drive through Idaho, but on the Jackson side, storm clouds were just starting to pour through the pass. The Tetons have fared relatively well in terms of snow recently and sit in a sweet spot that the latest NOAA models say might stay relatively snowy over the next 70 years. Still, 2012 was the warmest year in Wyoming history, and the snowline is clearly moving up.[29] Snowfall in the town of Jackson is down around seven percent over the last 50 years, and those numbers do not include the warm years of 2000–2013. Glaciers in the Wind River Range and Tetons have been receding and the state is funding cloud-seeding and snowmaking projects—including a grant to expand snowmaking at downtown Jackson's Snow King Resort.

Gaps in climate and snowfall data in the region have made long-term assessments difficult. Wyoming NOAA hydrologist Jim Fahey has been studying snowpack across the state since the 1990s and said the numbers on his end are pretty clear. "The snowpack from 7,500 to 11,000 feet has been below average since 1999, by 15 to 20 percent," he said. "It's warming up earlier in the spring, two to three weeks ahead of schedule. The snowpack calendar used to run from mid-October to the middle of May; now it's mid-November or early December to early May or late April. That's a month and a half to two months' less snow accumulation. That's a big deal. Call it global warming or whatever you want, but there is some kind of change happening with the climate. It's a whole new ball game."

The forecast called for nine inches of fresh by the next day, but everyone knew it would be more on the summit. That night the snow came in a white cloud, stacking up faster then snowplows could clear it. I met some friends I knew when I lived in Jackson to catch up. We reminisced about the thrill of being a twentysomething ski bum, standing outside the old Calico or the Mangy Moose, watching the snow come down and talking about what lines we'd ski in the morning. Not much had changed since then, as we chatted past midnight about life and work and then, inevitably, where the best powder would blow in the next day.

The next day was a Thursday, and the tram line was crammed with locals taking the morning off. It took 40 minutes to get on the lift, but it was worth it at the top. The tram operator told everyone to be careful and blasted heavy metal on the stereo as we ascended to the summit station. On the slope, I clicked into my skis and skated ahead of the crowd, then traversed Rendezvous Bowl to my favorite run down Far Drift. I'd skied the ridgeline hundreds of times, but it still took my breath away—accelerating downhill, the feeling of nothingness as my skis floated in the powder.

The frozen collar of my jacket chafed against my chin, and I tasted the metallic tang of snow on my tongue. It was hard to see through the face shots, but I could sense the great plume of crystals soaring down the mountain with me. I worked left toward the bowl and leaned forward into my boots over a short traverse. There was a line of bamboo poles up ahead, then an opening on the ridge. I slowed for a moment and slid over it. Then I pointed my skis down another steep shot and dropped back into the deep.

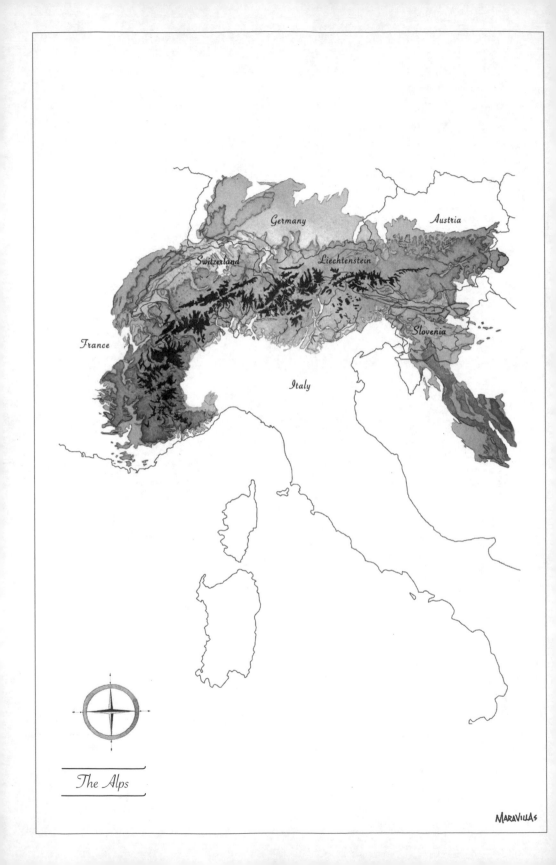

France

Switzerland

Germany

Liechtenstein

Austria

Slovenia

Italy

The Alps

MARAVILLAS

PART II

Jamie Pierre getting DEEP at Alta, Utah.

The Bald Bomber and friends take a break at Red Mountain's Deane Cabin, B.C.

Peter Velisek launches above Whitewater, B.C., with a freshly packed pipe.

The 4000 BC "Rødøy Hunter," discovered in 1929 in Norway.

Working out with the 10th Mountain Division.

Marilyn Monroe at a Sun Valley bus stop.

Kehr's Cabin at
Stevens Pass the
night of February
18, 2012.

Night-skiing lights
at Stevens Pass.

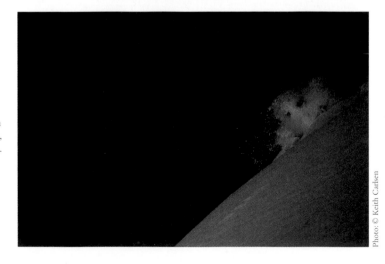

Jim Jack gets a
late-night face shot,
February 18, 2012.

The man with three
first names.

Photo: © Keith Carlsen

The bonfire outside Tim Wangen's
RV, February 18, 2012.

Photo: © Keith Carlsen

Powder goddess
Dolores LaChapelle.

Corey Felton drops
into Pacific Northwest
powder at Mount
Baker, Oregon.

Reading the future at the National Weather Service
Forecast Office, Portland, Oregon.

The road to Jackson Hole, Wyoming.

The next Shangri-la. Graham Land,
Antarctic Peninsula.

The Mer de Glace and Montenvers train in 2009. Chamonix, France.

The Mer de Glace in 1915. Chamonix, France.

J. J. 8847 Chamonix - Mer de Glace et chemin
de fer du Montenvers

Peter "PJ" Moran measures the crown of a 100-year avalanche on Mount Baker's Shuksan Arm.

Base camp before skiing Antarctica's Mount Shackleton.

Ski bum sketch-mobile at Big Sky, Montana.

Quest for the magic number. Biglow Canyon Wind Farm, The Dalles, Oregon.

Protecting our winters at Grand Targhee, Wyoming.

Photo: © Greg Von Doersten

Sammy Carlson throwing down in the Jackson Hole backcountry.

Dana Flahr night driving.

Keepin' it real with the Jackson Hole Air Force.

Photo: © Grant Gunderson

Photo: © Mattias Fredriksson

JACKSON HOLE
AIR FORCE

Photo: © Mattias Fredriksson

St. Anton local Stefan Häusl and Henrik
Windstedt pause above Stuben am Arlberg.

Photo: © Greg Von Doersten

The Master: Doug Coombs.

The "Goddess of l'Oisans," La Meije, La Grave, France.

Photo: © Mattias Fredriksson

Swiss Mister.
Rhone Valley,
Switzerland.

Finding the
rhythm in the
silver birch of
Niseko, Japan.

The thin red
line: 1907
avalanche map
of the Alps.
SLF, Davos,
Switzerland.

Jamie Pierre sets a world record at 255 feet.
Grand Targhee, Wyoming.

Chapter Ten
The Beast

Because it's there.

—*George Mallory*

This is a different place. The summits are too sheer to hold snow. Lower down, where the grade evens out, everything is white. Couloirs, cirques and snowfields drape into glacial valleys. The mountains are taller, the draws deeper. There are no trees in the high alpine, just a serpentine ridgeline of rockbound summits wandering away 25 miles north. Behind me, the tip of 15,781-foot Mont Blanc, the tallest peak in Europe, rises like a white whale. In front of me, the Grandes Jorasses and the Dent du Géant mark the Italian border. Beyond that lay the fairytale peaks of Switzerland: Monte Rosa, Breithorn, Matterhorn…

There are days up here when the wind blows 100 miles an hour and snow and ice stick to anything in their path. The afternoon I stepped off the Aiguille du Midi tram at 12,392 feet was not one of those days. I couldn't see a cloud from the summit dock. They were all down below, concealing the valley in a cottony carpet. A few stray cumulonimbus lingered around the smaller peaks and filled the tight gorges that brace the Mont Blanc massif. The sky was candy blue and the north wind so cold that my fingers went numb inside my gloves. The only sound: the whir of the tram as the bull wheel spun a half mile of cable down to Plan de l'Aiguille.

A few feet from the observation deck, a jet-black chough glided on a thermal. Its canary-yellow beak and red feet were the only color against the ivory landscape. Locals say the birds carry the souls of alpinists who have died in these mountains. Legendary skiers Anselme Baud, Patrick Vallençant and Trevor Petersen count among them. By the number of choughs circling the deck, the range seemed like a dangerous place. Indeed, Mont Blanc kills more climbers every year than Everest, the Matterhorn and Mount Denali combined.

My guide, Alfonso Pascual, tapped me on the shoulder and nodded at a line of people making their way down the Aiguille du Midi arête. The 49-year-old had a giant rope slung over his shoulder and wore a climbing harness. He is 5 foot 7, a Spaniard who grew up in Paris. Fifteen minutes ago, I'd learned that he is crazy, too—when he casually mentioned that, after reading Joshua Slocum's book *Sailing Alone Around the World*, he bought a 25-foot sailboat in Geneva and…sailed it around the world. It was the first time he'd ever piloted a boat. When he landed in the Canary Islands, his wife flew to meet him with an anchor in her backpack. "I realized I didn't have a way to stop," he said. Another self-imposed test: to see if he could ski the entire length of the Alps. He could. The only casualty was his relationship with an ex-girlfriend.

Alfonso moved to Chamonix not long after seeing the valley's icy peaks for the first time. It is no small thing to walk into the cradle of alpinism. The Mont Blanc massif lurches three vertical miles straight up from downtown. The Aiguilles Rouges mountains box the canyon in to the west. The Arve, the primary river of the upper Savoy, rushes, pale blue, from Col de Balme through town before joining the Rhone in Geneva. The border with Switzerland is nine miles to the north; Italy is nine to the south.

The valley is so narrow and deep—and only 10 miles long—that Chamonix gets just three hours of sunlight a day in the middle of winter. The town's name originates from the Latin term *campus munitus*, which means "fortified field" or "surrounded by walls." Locals simply call it the Dark Side. Or Death Valley. Or The Beast. Because more people die here recreating in the mountains than anywhere in the world.

Alfonso arrived as a climber, as many do, then quickly dove into the world of skiing. He attended the National School of Ski and Mountaineering in Chamonix—one of the most rigorous mountain-guide courses in the world—and has been guiding ever since. When he's not keeping people from dying in the mountains, he lives with his wife and four-year-old in a one-room studio in town.

We walked from the observation deck to the elevator. The shaft drops straight through the granite summit needle and connects, through a tunnel, to the knife-edge arête—which, in turn, leads to the upper reaches of the Vallée Blanche. Stepping past skiers rappelling hundreds of feet off suspended walkways, then through a passageway that pierces the heart of the mountain, is thrilling in a sick, IMAX kind of way. Except that the rocks are real and the cold is very real, and, out on the arête, nothing seems so real as the 6,000-foot plunge off the edge of the boot pack.

Alfonso donned crampons and meticulously coiled his rope, then handed me a harness. He clipped us together and we walked through a tunnel bored through the summit glacier. It hadn't snowed in two weeks and the chiseled stairs down the arête had melted into a frozen sluice. I was wearing three-year-old ski boots with worn-out soles, and every step felt like creeping down a luge course in slippers. Once a year, someone slips on the path and meets his or her maker thousands of feet below.

We took the upper section slowly, slowed further by a man who had clipped a short rope from his harness to the guideline—and had to awkwardly unclip and reattach it at each post. The guideline itself was covered in ice and impossible to grip. Even though I was tied to Alfonso, I was almost twice his size and didn't want to imagine the tumble we'd take if I went down. The wind blew 40 miles an hour over the ridge, making the wind chill -60 degrees Fahrenheit. Halfway down, Alfonso told me to cover my left cheek. By the time we reached the start of the Vallée Blanche, I had a two-inch dark-brown streak of frostbite across my cheekbone.

Below us, a great white sheet of snow and ice rippled through a breach in the mountains. The Vallée Blanche Classique skiing route runs skier's left of the nose-like Gros Rognon rock to a giant serac field, the Tacul Glacier and, eventually, the Mer de Glace Glacier, which wraps around almost to Chamonix. From end to end the run is 12 miles long and drops 9,000 vertical feet. It is the most famous off-piste ski slope in the Alps and one of the longest, with 80,000 people skiing it every year. It is also a schuss through the history of alpinism, skiing and mountain travel—which began here two and a half centuries ago.

Written history of the "Vallée de Chamouny" appears in 1091, when a count from Genevois gifted the valley to Benedictine monks of the Abbey Saint-Michel de la Cluse near Turin, Italy. The monks established a priory there, but avalanches, snow and inclement weather gave the region a dangerous reputation and kept most people away. Civil and church officials were the only outside visitors until citizens were granted the right to hold public fairs in the 16th century and a few peddlers wandered up the banks of the Arve.

Leisure travelers were rare in those times. Mountain goers were nearly nonexistent. To the few souls living near them, the high peaks were to be avoided. The Raetians and Gauls of the Roman period depicted demons in the summits in their epigraphs. Later, the Alemanni of the seventh century and scribes of the Habsburg Empire embossed images on book jackets of icy fiends hiding in the peaks. During Alpine festivals, villagers made loud noises and built fires to chase evil spirits away, and it was common practice for passengers to be blindfolded when travelling over mountain passes.

It wasn't until the Age of Enlightenment that people started exploring the mountains—mostly wealthy intellectuals using "scientific methods" to understand unexplained ways of the world. (Leonardo da Vinci predated the trend, climbing to a snowfield near Monte Rosa in the 1400s to make scientific observations.) Two such explorers, William Windham and Richard Pococke, spotted the white mass of Mont Blanc in 1741 from the streets of Geneva. Windham had just undertaken a grand tour of Europe and Pococke had recently returned from an expedition to Egypt. The pair secured guides, packhorses, provisions, a tent and firearms and set out on June 19 for Chamonix—rumor has it with Pococke in full Arabian dress.[30]

The group spent a few days following the Arve, visiting small villages and firing off their pistols in mountain passes to "test the acoustics" of the echoes that reverberated back. In Chamonix, they finally spotted the icy tongues of the glaciers they'd come to inspect. Against the admonitions of the local priori, the pair hired peasants to guide them into the mountains to see the great white beasts for themselves.[31]

The only people scrambling up the rocky flanks of the Alps at the time were chamois and crystal hunters—the latter seeking cinnabar, amethyst and quartz—so finding a guide wasn't easy. The duo eventually did and the expedition set out the next day, using long walking poles with steel tips and making frequent stops to drink water mixed with wine. Five hours later, they reached the summit and beheld a sight so extraordinary it inspired a migration to the mountains for centuries to come.[32] As Windham wrote:

> Our Road lay slantways, and we had several Places to cross where the *Avalanches* of Snow were fallen, and had made terrible Havock; there was nothing to be seen but Trees torn up by the Roots, and large Stones, which seemed to live without any Support; every step we set, the Ground gave way, the Snow which was mixed with it made us slip, and had it not been for our Staffs, and our Hands, we must many times have gone down the Precipice. We had an uninterrupted View quite to the Bottom of the Mountain, and the Steepness of the Descent, join'd to the Height where we were, made a View terrible enough to make most People's Heads turn. In short, after climbing with great Labor for four Hours and three

Quarters, we got to the Top of the Mountain; from whence we had the Pleasure of beholding Objects of an extraordinary Nature. We were on the Top of a Mountain, which, as well as we could judge, was at least twice as high as the mount *Saleve*, from thence we had a full View of the *Glaciers*. I own to you that I'm extremely at a Loss how to give the right Idea of it; as I know no one thing which I have ever seen that has the least Resemblance to it.[33]

The group returned to Chamonix that night and, a few days later, to Geneva. Soon after arriving home in England, they made presentations of their trip, describing 40-foot crests of frozen water and bottomless blue crevasses in what they called the Mer de Glace (Sea of Ice). Word of the account spread quickly, and by the following year the tiny farming village of Chamonix—rather surprised and unprepared—received its first tourists.

The Vallée Blanche looked more like a frozen river than an ocean as Alfonso and I made our first turns down. To skier's left, the gnarled granite fingers of Mont Maudit and the Aiguille Verte cut through the sky. To the south we could see Italy and the top of the Helbronner lift, which connects to the outskirts of Courmayeur. To skier's right, Alfonso pointed out the Gervasutti Couloir, etched into the east face of Mont-Blanc du Tacul—and the shimmering bulge of black ice near the top, where Hans Saari fell to his death in 2001.

There are two other main routes besides the Classique down the Vallée Blanche. The Grand Envers du Plan tracks high left through couloirs and serac fall before dropping to the Glacier du Géant. The Petit Envers follows a mellow line in between that and the Classique. The Grand Envers du Plan was the *real* Vallée Blanche, Alfonso said, so we headed left to ski it.

The snow was scoured by wind at the top, and we cut around a long ridge to find something more sheltered. The powder there was cold and light and lifted around our knees as we picked up speed. Alfonso skied a line close to a deep-blue crevasse and a few seracs the size of small houses. "The closer you get to the cracks, the better the powder!" he yelled.

Down below, he pointed out the Salle à Manger—translation: "Dining Room"—where skiers traditionally stop for lunch. It had changed drastically over the years as the glacier melted, he said. There were too many crevasses to stop there now. He then pointed to the Envers du Plan Glacier that used to collide with the Tacul. They hadn't touched in years, he said, as the Envers du Plan had receded hundreds of meters uphill.

We followed a crosscut to the Refuge du Requin, a small cabin clinging to the side of an escarpment. The refuge was built by hand in 1924 as the first-night's accommodations on the hike to Mont Blanc. Ski guide Roland Couttet sat next to us and told us that he'd been guiding in Chamonix since he was 18. Which was in 1962. The 69-year-old's hands were like worn leather gloves and his face was wrinkled and tanned. He'd been enjoying powder all winter, he said, but even with the new snow, the Vallée Blanche was nothing like the old days.

It used to snow a meter at a time in town, he recalled. He had to shovel his family's walkway every day, December through March. In the summer, he said, the "glacier" that the Classique route follows around the Géant serac fall isn't a glacier at all. It's rock and dirt. As is the trail back to Chamonix, he advised Alfonso, suggesting that we take the Montenvers train down instead.

We wished Roland well and skied to Salle à Manger, where a few intrepid groups sat on their gear and ate baguettes layered with thick slices of brie and *saucisson*. Alfonso told me to stay in his tracks as he weaved around 30-story-deep crevasses. Every year, the peaceful scene turns deadly when someone unknowingly falls into one, he said. We made long, slow turns, then followed a single track over the flat expanse of the Mer de Glace. On the right, the Leschaux Glacier twisted up to the golden rock walls of the Grandes Jorasses. It was early afternoon and flaxen light touched the granite spire of the Dru and the 11,000-foot ridgeline of the

Aiguille du Moine. The Mer de Glace hooked left and we dropped into a glacial runnel for a bobsled run to the foot of the glacier.

We stopped and Alfonso pointed up to the Montenvers train. Since 1908, the railway has transported visitors to the Mer de Glace. I could see the red cars and oversized panorama windows from where we stood. Just below the observation deck, high above the glacier, was a giant flat rock. Windham and Pococke ate there before returning to Chamonix, Alfonso said. "The top of the glacier used to be there," he said.

His expression lingered somewhere between confused and frightened. In the last century the Mer de Glace has thinned by 590 feet and receded a mile and a half up the valley.[34] Every summer, Alfonso hikes from town to add rungs to a ladder leading from the Refuge du Requin down to the glacier. In the last 25 years, he's had to lengthen the ladder 250 feet. "They're going to build a walkway to the glacier that goes almost a mile up the valley," he said, "because that's where it's going to end in a few years."

The amount of ice that has vanished from the Mer de Glace in the last century is hard to put into words; imagine lower Manhattan sinking 600 feet beneath the ocean. Throughout the Alps, scientists have seen much of the same. The range is warming three times faster than the global average and, overall, has lost half of its glacial ice in the last century—20 percent of that since the 1980s. Where 75 percent of Alpine glaciers were advancing in 1980, 90 percent are now retreating.[35] Switzerland alone has lost a fifth of its glacial surface area in the past 15 years—including 1,000 glaciers that have vanished—and it's possible that the continent could be almost completely glacier-free as soon as 2050.[36]

What that means for skiing is obvious. Recent studies suggest that on the planet's current track, two-thirds of all ski areas in Europe will no longer be snow-reliable in 50 to 70 years.[37] Considering the importance of the sport in European culture and the amount of water the Alps provide to the continent, the potential loss of snow and ice there threatens everything from economies to food availability to national identities. The fact that the Alps will likely be the first major skiing range in the world to melt out, also means skiers and industry executives in the

U.S. are watching closely to see how Europeans adapt and try to stop it.

Standing at the foot of the Mer de Glace, the thought of an Alpine scene without snow-capped mountains was hard to imagine. Pictures of the Matterhorn and Eiger—in addition to those of ski pioneers like Hannes Schneider and Émile Allais—have come to symbolize mountain life and adventure around the world. With so much history packed into the range, an ice-free Europe seemed like something from a science fiction novel.

In fact, in 1816 it was 18-year-old Mary Shelley, in her book *Frankenstein*, who best described the awe of the high Alps. Shelley visited Chamonix in *la belle saison*, at the end of July. She and her new husband, Percy Shelley, didn't have an easy time getting there. Heavy rain turned them back one day, and Percy knocked himself out after slipping on a rock. After they finally reached the glacier, Mary added to her book the greatest description of what is at stake in the high peaks of Europe:

> From the side where I now stood Montanvert was exactly opposite, at the distance of a league; and above it rose Mont Blanc, in awful majesty. I remained in a recess of the rock, gazing on this wonderful and stupendous scene. The sea, or rather the vast river of ice, wound among its dependent mountains, whose aerial summits hung over its recesses. Their icy and glittering peaks shone in the sunlight over the clouds. My heart, which was before sorrowful, now swelled with something like joy; I exclaimed, "Wandering spirits, if indeed ye wander, and do not rest in your narrow beds, allow me this faint happiness, or take me, as your companion, away from the joys of life."

Chapter Eleven

A Castle of Many Rivers

The true skier does not follow where others lead. He is not confined to a piste. He is an artist who creates a pattern of lovely lines from virgin and uncorrupted snow. What marble is to the sculptor, so are the latent harmonies of ridge and hollow, powder, and sun-softened crust to the true skier. By a wise dispensation of providence, the snow, whose beauty has been defaced and destroyed by the multitude of piste addicts, does not record the passage of the "lifted skier." It is only soft snow that records the movements of individual skiers, and it is only in soft snow that the real artist can express himself.

—*Sir Arnold Lunn*

In September 1991, in the Ötztal Alps of Italy—200 miles northeast of Chamonix—two German hikers discovered a corpse. Erika and Helmut Simon were descending Finail Peak in the Tisenjoch region when they followed a shortcut and spotted the body. It was half-buried, its chest leaning against a flat rock. Two rolled pieces of birch bark lay beside it.

The cadaver was discovered 10,500 feet above the valley floor and was almost perfectly preserved, along with much of its clothing and possessions. Forensic experts and archeologists deduced that the man lived in the Copper Age, between 3350 and 3100 BC. He was a man of some means and was around 46 years old. He was wearing a woven grass cloak, a leather loincloth and a bearskin cap with a chinstrap and was armed with a dagger, a bow, a quiver of dogwood arrows and a copper-tipped axe. In a pouch sewn into his belt, he had flakes of flint and fire-starting material. The man had been shot in the back with an arrow and, after piling his personal possessions next to him, sat down in the snow and died. He had not gone easily. The blood of four other men was found on his clothes.

"Ötzi the Iceman" taught scientists several important lessons about ancient history. One was the fact that travelers crossed the Alps well before the Romans, and that those who did knew how to dress, navigate and survive in cold weather. Another was that the paths they used through high mountain passes were once largely ice-free. Lastly, Ötzi's preserved body showed climatologists that the Alps were blanketed with snow and ice soon after his death and stayed that way for 5,000 years—until recently, when they started to melt.

Temperature swings are not unique to Earth. Scientists need only look to our neighbors to see similar fluctuations—and understand the consequences of extreme heating or cooling. Venus underwent a radical greenhouse effect that boiled its oceans and left most of its carbon suspended in a stifling blanket in the atmosphere. Mars suffered the opposite fate: the planet was once temperate with abundant water, but somehow most of its carbon ended up in the ground, and the planet froze.[38]

Over the millennia Earth somehow regulated itself, making climate swings milder. Seven hundred million years ago, the planet was covered in ice. Sixty million years ago, when dinosaurs wandered the poles, there wasn't a shard of ice to be found. Modern history has seen smaller fluctuations. The years between 1860 and 1910 saw substantial cooling, then warming between 1910 and 1943, followed by another cooling period. The most recent radical cooling event, known as the Little Ice Age, took place from 1500 to 1850 and significantly impacted life in the Northern Hemisphere. Growing seasons contracted in northern Europe, causing grain prices to skyrocket, widespread famine and subsequent conflicts like the Thirty Years' War. The average height of Europeans dropped an inch in the 1500s due to malnourishment, and in Iceland the population fell by half. [39]

Glaciers in the Alps grew considerably during the Little Ice Age. Entire villages in Switzerland were wiped out by the slow-moving ice, as well as valuable grazing pasture. The villages of Bonnenuit, Le Châtelard and La Bonneville in the Chamonix Valley were razed. When the Mer de Glace encroached on Les Bois in the 1700s, villagers brought in a bishop and marched to the foot of the glacier, singing hymns and praying.

The bishop sprinkled holy water on the ice and blessed it, and residents erected a statue of Saint Ignatius in its path. The glacier didn't stop and Les Bois was evacuated in 1825, though the village was never destroyed. For comparison, the temperature shift that initiated the Little Ice Age was between 1 and 2 degrees Celsius.[40] Which explains why scientists like Dr. Luc Moreau have been trying to figure out what the rapid melting of Europe's glaciers foretells.

For a glaciologist, Moreau is a bit of a swashbuckler: silver hair, broad smile, equal parts Indiana Jones and Anderson Cooper. He arrived in Chamonix in 1987 and graduated from the Grenoble Alpine Geography Institute in 1995. He makes frequent television appearances describing glacial dynamics and consults with a power company that makes hydro-electricity from runoff beneath the Mer de Glace. A self-proclaimed "glacionaut," he explores ice caves and hidden glacial wells on televised *Nova* expeditions and for his own research. He is also a glacier guide for the Compagnie du Mont-Blanc, the enterprise that operates the train and most of the lifts in Chamonix.

I met Moreau in the Montenvers train station the day after skiing the Vallée Blanche. His black-and-white speckled dog, Poppy, trotted behind him. The station was built in the early 1900s and looked like not much had been altered since then: brass fixtures, gaslights, the original Number Six steam locomotive that hauled tourists to the Mer de Glace. Photos in the station show men in suit vests and work boots digging tunnels through solid rock with pickaxes and shovels and positioning giant slabs of granite into arched bridges. Another series shows men in derby hats and women in bonnets boarding the rack-and-adhesion railway alongside gendarmes to climb 2,858 vertical feet to one of the great wonders of the world.

Moreau explained how a glacier works from the pine-slatted seats of the car, Poppy curled at his feet. Glaciers are essentially rivers of ice. Accumulation zones in the Alps are located around 10,000 feet or higher, where snow collects faster than it melts. Above 13,000 feet, the average temperature is below freezing and snow and ice adhere to the rock they rest on. At around 12,000 feet, ice softens near the freezing point and the weight of the glacier makes it slide downhill, cracking in the process and opening up crevasses.

Moreau smiles a lot when he talks about ice, until we talk about what has been happening recently, and what will happen if the planet continues to warm. He is hesitant to speculate too far into the future, perhaps—like many people I spoke with in the Alps—because his livelihood depends on it. But he is a scientist first and knows the facts. The temperature spike in the last 20 years alone has thinned the Mer de Glace extensively, largely because of abnormally hot summers. Its flow also has dropped, from 300 feet per year in 1980 to 115 feet per year in 2009.[41] "If the glacier continues to retreat, it can go back to the point where it was 6,000 and 8,000 years ago," he says. "But at that time it was completely natural, which is the difference with today."

In the world of climate change, melting glaciers are the canary in the coal mine. But every region and elevation in the Alps is being affected. The average temperature in Annecy, France, is more than 2 degrees Fahrenheit warmer today than it was a century ago. Chamonix is nearly 3 degrees Fahrenheit warmer, and snow accumulation in the area has dropped by 50 percent in the last 40 years, mostly at lower elevations. In the last 50 years, the amount of snow below 3,000 feet in the Alps is down 40 percent and the freezing level has moved up 650 vertical feet. Most of the change has happened since the 1960s, but the highest rate of change has risen dramatically since the 1990s.[42]

The train stopped at Montenvers Station and we got off behind an American woman, cloaked in furs, who insisted that no one told her this was her stop. "It's the only stop," a man traveling with her said, pointing to a pile of snow at the end of the tracks. Moreau grinned and cheerily said hello. Then he threw a shard of ice for Poppy to retrieve and everyone on the platform laughed. Behind him the great void of the Mer de Glace wound up to the Vallée Blanche. This year, everything was white: the glacier, the peaks, the craggy ridgelines bracing them. Tourists milled around the observation deck, reading placards that described the mechanics of a glacier.

Moreau likes to explain that ice in the Mer de Glace directly below the observation deck fell in Paris as rain in the early 1800s—and gas bubbles trapped in the foot of the glacier are filled with air dating back to the French Revolution. The glacier's retreat is harder to convey, and in the future, he said, it's only going to get more difficult. Every year, the Mer de Glace recedes 100 to 130 feet. So in 40 years it will melt almost a mile back to the first bend of the canyon—not coincidentally where the Compagnie du Mont-Blanc is building its new walkway. If the temperature rises 4 degrees Celsius, the glacier would essentially vanish, except for a few pieces of the Géant clinging to the summit of Mont Blanc. If that were to happen, Moreau said, skiing and sightseeing would be the least of Europe's worries. Without the "Water Tower of Europe," he said, the continent would be in trouble.

"The Alps are a castle of many rivers for Europe," he said. "It's a very important problem for the future because the river is life. Millions of people in Europe live from it....We live with this nature; we live with this glacier, with this tree, with this animal. It is the composition of our life, like the fish in the sea, like all of these elements, and we are very happy to see this. We must adapt. Very quickly."

Moreau pointed out moraines high on the valley walls that mark where the glacier used to be. Then, almost a mile above that, he showed me ridgelines the ice rounded during the last Ice Age. Across the valley he pointed to the Dru, the most famous climb in Chamonix. The route the first climber used to get up the granite spire is no longer there, he said. The permafrost that held the massive vertical slabs together melted and the side of the mountain fell off.

We looked down at the rock where Windham and Pococke dined and Moreau said that a family of marmots lived there now. Far below that, beyond the foot of the glacier, the valley was brown and scattered with boulders, icefall, muddy streams and decaying trees. The ridgelines twisted left, then right, then left again where the Mer de Glace carved them thousands of years ago. Closer to the valley floor, where a new forest had cropped up, there was no snow at all.

I walked the streets of Chamonix that afternoon under broad, low-angle chalet roofs—designed centuries ago to gather snow for insulation. Across a stone bridge spanning the Arve, I smelled chimney smoke on the tiny Rue des Moulins. A group of young ski mountaineers with faded Gore-Tex jackets and climbing harnesses still on sat in a steamy sandwich shop, devouring baguettes filled with meat and veggies. On the sidewalk, a voguish couple sipped *vin chaud* at an outdoor stand—all the while, the constant presence of massive white mountains hovering above.

Chamonix is still an old place. There are chamois hunters who climb the hills and a horseman in traditional shearling who carries tourists down Ravanel le Rouge in his carriage. Napoleon III planned the roads that crisscross the town, and many haven't changed since. The bell tower of the St. Michel church is 1,000 years old. Near the arched doorway, just before the stairs, tiny skiers are melted into the church's stained-glass windows.

The day I arrived, I watched a half dozen pallbearers carry the coffin of a mountain-rescue gendarme past those windows and out the door. He'd fallen into a crevasse during a training exercise. The coffin was draped with a French flag. The 40-year-old's wife and two children followed it out as three rescue helicopters buzzed the square.

Tiny flakes spindled through the darkening sky into the glow of streetlights when I walked through Place Balmat. Jacques Balmat and Dr. Michel-Gabriel Paccard were the first to climb Mont Blanc in 1786, sparking a rush on Europe's high peaks that culminated in the Golden Age of Alpinism in the mid-1800s—when 100 Alpine first ascents were logged. Steam swirled around restaurants and nightclubs just opening their shades, while trinket shops and crêperies rolled down their gates for the night. The first drunken Swedes of the evening stumbled past, followed by four even drunker Brits, then a gang of French teenage boys wearing skinny jeans and long, curly hair. The old mountaineers were long gone by then. They'd already eaten dinner and were probably getting ready for bed.

I crossed back over the river on another bridge and knocked on the door of Chamonix Météo, where Yan Giezendanner buzzed me in. Giezendanner is known as "The Weather God" to serious alpinists.

Multiple sclerosis has confined him to a wheelchair, so he forecasts the weather for climbers everywhere from Chamonix to Mount Everest Base Camp from his apartment or the Météo offices.

Giezendanner's gray-streaked hair falls to the top of his back and his lanky upper body moves slowly and gracefully. He's called the weather in Chamonix since 1975 and told me about weather trends over the last four decades. Most big snowstorms come from the southern shores of Greenland and Iceland, where warm water from the Atlantic and cold water from the Arctic converge. Recently, though, a strong flow from the south has been predominant. The southern blasts bring plenty of snow, but they can transport warm air, too. He said that although there has been more snow on the valley floor recently, it's not as much as there was 30 or 40 years ago. As far as the end of snow and skiing by the end of the century, though, he didn't buy it. Everything fluctuates all the time, he said, and the current warming trend is no different.

"For me it is just a cycle," he said. "The next 10 to 20 years, it is difficult to say. But for me, climate change is probably big propaganda. The last century and the ones before, it was warm. You have a model and a calculator of 50 years, but it is always artificial. It is very difficult."

Giezendanner said that it was just too soon to tell exactly what was warming the Earth and how long it would continue. The causes could be greenhouse gases, sunspots, Arctic currents, the jet stream or the Gulf Stream, among others. The Earth was warm in the Middle Ages and cooler during the Little Ice Age. The parameters of forecasting weather are simply too complex for science to know what will happen in 80 years. "For me, it's a young science—too young," he said. "Some big teachers at university say climate change is not true. Green-washing is big business, you know?"

I thought about Giezendanner's perspective the next day as I rode the lift at Les Grands Montets. Grands Montets is the largest of Chamonix's five resorts, with three mountains and nearly 4,500 acres of skiing terrain. It started to rain when I loaded onto the summit tram. Sixty skiers piled in and the box took off. It wasn't a full house; it was midweek and it hadn't snowed for a while. The clouds were so thick on the ride up that I couldn't see the slope below. Halfway to the top, the tram burst through a cloud layer into clear blue sky. The peaks and glaciers and mile-wide slopes all around looked like a scene in a snow globe. Below, a pillow of clouds spread over the valley, leaving only the tips of the tallest peaks poking through.

The view was so striking that I had to blink a couple of times to believe it. Ten inches of fresh powder covered every run, with a few curvy tracks cut through them. I spent a half hour taking pictures on the summit station before climbing down four flights of metal stairs and clicking into my skis. A few skiers ducked under a rope marking off uncontrolled glacial terrain and I did exactly what you're not supposed to and followed them. The run rolled over into a steep headwall, edged on the right by sapphire-blue seracs and a rocky face. I skied to the right of the couple ahead of me through a field of fresh snow. I made a few tight turns, then carved back and forth in wide, sweeping arcs. There was so much room, so much white all around, it felt like I could ski in any direction and never stop.

I made 50 turns to a groomed trail and another 50 back to the tram—then repeated the same run all afternoon, practically alone as the clouds peeled back and a cerulean sky reached down to the Aiguille Rouge. When the lift closed, I followed the right side of the glacier to Pointe du Vue and the Refuge de Lognan. The stone building was set on a hillock below the Argentière Glacier icefalls. During World War II it was a barracks, but now it serves food and keeps rooms for guests. If emissions continue to rise and long-term forecasts are accurate, the mid-mountain refuge will sit close to the snowline in 2100.

An old French record played in the café and I sat on a stone wall outside and listened. I could hear silverware and glasses clinking and smell melted cheese on a plate of *tartiflette*. A black Labrador sniffed around the foundation of the building, and three young French girls with frizzy hair and headbands walked out in their ski boots—through a rickety door with a note pinned to it: "Ferme la porte!"

The scene was from another time, when expats and Europeans wedeled on hickory boards through virgin powder and listened to Lucienne Boyer on vinyl in the lodge. It reminded me of my grandparents, who were ski fanatics and probably ate at the Lognan. I envisioned their creased stretch pants and the yellow Smith goggles they used to wear. It seemed like things were less complicated then. But that is nostalgia talking. Before my grandfather ever skied the Alps, he fought in World War II in Europe— and saw things that he never spoke about again. As alpenglow moved up the steep mountainsides and more guests poured out of the refuge for their last run, it dawned on me that every generation has its fight.

Chapter Twelve
La Meije

Everything is flowing—going somewhere, animals and so-called lifeless rocks as well as water. Thus the snow flows fast or slow in grand beauty-making glaciers and avalanches; the air in majestic floods carrying minerals, plant leaves, seeds, spores, with streams of music and fragrance; water streams carrying rocks....While the stars go streaming through space pulsed on and on forever like blood...in Nature's warm heart.

—*John Muir,* My First Summer in the Sierra, *1911*

The Alps are tall, but they are not big. From end to end, the range is just over 750 miles long, arcing in a boomerang around the cuff of Italy's boot. The mountains are part of the ancient Alpide belt, which begins in Gibraltar and hooks east and south through the Carpathians and Himalayas to peaks in Southeast Asia. In all, the Alps cover just 80,000 square miles, an area a bit smaller than the state of Kansas.

A few days after skiing Les Grand Montets, I headed south out of Chamonix on a month-long tour of the range. If melting in the region was a harbinger of things to come, I wanted to get a glimpse of what the future of snow looked like. The southern route out of Chamonix follows the western hook of the boomerang and passes through the heart of French ski country. I merged onto Route Blanche early in the morning and drove past the entrance of the infamous Mont Blanc Tunnel—where, in 1999, a Belgian truck carrying flour and margarine started a blaze that killed 39 people, including a local Chamonix fireman. The tunnel was in the news again recently. Chamonix authorities were planning to ban the most polluting freight trucks that pass through it, to cut emissions in the valley—which some thought were affecting temperatures and snowfall there. Town officials had also reduced speed limits and proposed reopening the Saint Gervais-Vallorcine train line to shuttle visitors and reduce emissions.

The road followed the Arve for 15 miles before banking south to Saint-Gervais-les-Bains and the historic ski village of Megève. Megève wasn't the first ski town in the Alps—St. Moritz and Davos usually get that distinction—but it was the first purpose-built ski *resort*. Noémie de Rothschild broke ground in Megève after becoming disenchanted with St. Moritz. Her plan was to transform the tiny farming hamlet into a more civilized ski-centric destination. Her first project, in 1924, was the extravagant Chalet du Mont d'Arbois, and by the end of the next winter Megève was the winter resort of choice for European aristocrats.

Megève was home to many early ski innovations, like stretch pants with stirrups and progressive ski design—the latter thanks to local ski champion Émile Allais and Abel Rossignol. Rothschild made history again when she hired architect Henry-Jacques Le Même to design a private house for her. Le Même admired the broad double roof and agrarian aesthetic of local farmhouses and incorporated them into Rothschild's home. The result effectively transformed the word *chalet*, which until then meant "farmer's hut," into *chalet du skieur*, a design that spread almost as quickly through the Alps as Megève's trendy reputation.

The resort touted its low elevation and less-demanding runs in the early days—attracting well-heeled skiers who didn't want to risk crevasses or avalanches. As Nadine de Rothschild wrote in her memoir, *Megève, Un Roman d'Amour*, "its medium altitude, its gentle climate and slopes. In Megève nothing is rude, nothing is abrupt, everything evokes feminine charm." Driving through that day, I saw the mild climate had affected something else—namely the amount of snow on the trails.

Low clouds covered the high peaks the morning I drove past the ski hill's lower slopes, which were half white and half brown with large swaths of grass showing through. There wasn't any snow in the trees or on chalet roofs. Chairlifts glided over brown fields, which looked more like pasture than trails. It was surprising to see, considering that the winter of 2012–2013 was one of Europe's biggest in years. But the resort is one of the lower ones in the Alps and its base area, at 3,444 feet, sits below the projected snowline for mid-century.

The road plummeted practically straight down near the outskirts of town, along the Arly River. Warm air washed through the car as I piloted around arching stone bridges and through narrow tunnels. On the valley floor, the highway cleaved through the thick forests and farmland surrounding Albertville, host of the 1992 Olympics. I passed the monolithic cliffs of Chartreuse soon after, where Carthusian monks have been making the herbal liquor that bears the mountains' name since the 1740s, then arrived in Grenoble, the "Capital of the Alps." The city is set at the confluence of the Isère and Drac rivers, near the village where Abel Rossignol built some of the first skis in France for the French Army. He used American hickory and European ash and tested the boards a few hours down the road in Briançon, site of the world's first ski school in 1903.

South of Grenoble, I breached the first peaks of the Southern Alps, which include the subranges Hautes-Alpes, Alpes de Haute Provence and Alpes-Maritimes. I noticed hints of Mediterranean influence in the towns of Vizille and Allemond: arched Romanesque doorways, rounded roof tiles and *génoise* friezes painted under the eaves. The Mediterranean influences the weather in the Southern Alps as well. The range sees significantly more sunny days than the north. There are fewer storms, too, but the ones that hit resorts like La Grave, Les Deux Alpes and Serre Chevalier tend to carry loads of precipitation from the sea and dump meters of snow at a time. With a dominant southwesterly flow in 2013, the range had seen a tremendous winter so far—making the world's greatest freeride mountain that much greater by the time I arrived.

There is a prelude to arriving in La Grave, as if the mountains are setting you up for something. After the flats of Albertville and Grenoble, where hulking massifs exist in the distance, the peaks in the Romanche Valley close in around you like skyscrapers lining a Manhattan avenue. Route N91 shadows the Romanche River and is the width of a trailer home, with a 50-story drop-off on the right-hand shoulder. Sometimes there's a guardrail, sometimes not.

Ten minutes into the drive, it started to snow. Ten minutes after that, it started to snow hard. There was no traffic, and the thought crossed my mind as I eased around the edge of a bottomless precipice that I was driving to a dead end. Then I turned another corner and glimpsed a post office, a church and a handful of slate-roofed houses seemingly suspended in the middle of the sky.

Until France annexed the House of Savoy in 1792—and Mont Blanc with it—the Parc National des Écrins that abuts La Grave boasted the highest peak in the country: 13,458-foot Barre des Écrins. With more than 100 summits taller than 3,000 meters, the region was one of France's early centers for mountaineering, attracting world-renowned climbers like Edward Whymper and Michel Croz. The "Goddess of l'Oisans," 13,081-foot La Meije—home of La Grave's ski resort—was the goal of many expeditions, but remained, until 1877, one of the last great peaks in Europe to be summited.

In 1894, a doctor hatched a proposal to build a 50-bed hospital for respiratory patients on the summit of La Meije, accessed by an underground funicular. The plan, along with several others, failed, and the mountain remained untouched until 1978, when a two-stage pulse gondola—for summer hikers and sightseers—was completed. When the lift was first opened for the winter a few years later, a new era of ski history began.

Many of the early skiers in La Grave migrated from Chamonix in the late 1980s. As diverse and challenging as Chamonix's terrain was, the hyper-competitive, egotistic scene there turned off some serious alpinists. Swedish guide and freeski champion Pele Lång was one of the first migrants, followed by a crew of iconic ski bums like the Crud Brothers: Vermont Bill and Jay Bird. Lång eventually bought into a larch-sided hostel above La Grave called La Chaumine. For a decade, the hostel hosted the best skiers in the world, who ventured to "Valley X" to test themselves on La Meije. Some made a life skiing here; many others died trying.

I spotted the swooping cables of the gondola as I drove into town. They rise 5,742 vertical feet and, with a T-bar, access more than 7,000 vertical feet of skiing on La Meije. The resort is a classic DIY Alpine area, with no ski patrol, few marked trails and no avalanche control. You simply get on the lift and find your way down. Five glaciers—the Râteau, Vallon, Girose, Tabuchet and La Meije—flow down the mountain, and the couloirs and cirques tucked in and around them offer everything from powder runs to death-defying 60-degree steeps. The four Trifides Couloirs are some of the most popular—and deadly—with around 800 vertical feet of 45- to 55-degree slopes. (More than three dozen people have died in the Trifides alone.) Les Couloirs du Lac feed down to a kettle lake skier's left of the gondola, and, off the Girose drag lift, skiers can drop into full-on mountaineering routes like the Orcières, Maison Neuve, Chirouze and Girose.

The storm was a whiteout when I parked outside the Hotel Edelweiss. I got vertigo for a moment when I stepped out of the car and looked practically straight down thousands of feet to the Romanche River. A few skiers walked up N91 through the snow, and I met a few more waxing their boards in the hotel's tuning room. Guests in the hotel bar that night chatted quietly about the weather, avalanches and three cars that drove off N91 that day. I checked the forecast online before going to bed and saw the brewing maelstrom was going to be a whopper. The barometer had dropped to 987 hPa, and a massive front—which enveloped much of Europe—was slowing down over the Alps. What that meant for La Grave was lots of snow—and lots of avalanches.

Morning comes haltingly in the Romanche Valley as the sun eases over the Massif des Écrins. The local TV news channel showed French soldiers restoring power to 80,000 homes affected by the blizzard. Two feet or more had buried most of Europe, creating 1,000 miles of traffic jams in Belgium alone. At the summit station of La Grave, five feet of new snow had fallen.

Local skier and international ski bum Ptor Spricenieks was caked with powder when he met me that morning at the hotel. Ptor and I had been on a few ski mountaineering trips in South America years before, and he'd offered to show me around La Grave. He lives near the La Chaumine in the satellite village of Ventelon with his wife, Karin, and two children—and had skied down the terraced hillside that morning. To friends, Ptor is a six-foot-two space alien from the planet Shred who landed on Earth millennia ago to ski the highest, steepest peaks in the world. He keeps his frizzy brown hair in a ponytail, and his Roman nose, well, beats all Roman noses of all time.

Ptor hails from a long line of psychedelic ski bums who cut their teeth in Whistler, British Columbia, in the 1980s. He followed a similar path that many young ski lions did then: competing in the third World Extreme Skiing Championships in Alaska, shredding with the Crud Brothers at Stevens Pass and eventually landing in La Grave. It hadn't snowed on La Meije for weeks before the storm, he said, and all of the new snow spiked avalanche danger to five on a scale of five. Ten skiers had died in the Haute-Alpes in the last week—almost all from avalanches—and the "commission" of guides that determines whether La Grave will open or not had decided that it would not. At least for today.

We played it safe and headed to Briançon instead to get groceries and speak with a photographer who'd been shooting glaciers around La Grave for 50 years. Jean Louis Francou met us at the door of Photo Francou wearing a black V-neck sweater, dark slacks and steel-rimmed glasses. With thinning gray hair combed straight back, he looked like an alpine version of Henri Cartier-Bresson. In fact, Francou's grandmother bought the business from another early 20th-century French photographer, named Chautard. Francou brought out some of Chautard's large-format slides shot in the 1920s. The grainy images were of guides in wide-brimmed hats and tall leather boots, perched on the Noir and Blanc glaciers in the Parc des Écrins. Behind the guides, in one photo, clients in three-piece suits crawled over a wooden ladder spanning a gaping crevasse.

Francou's family name goes back to the 1400s in Briançon. He took his first picture on January 1, 1964, on a glacier. "So I had to learn to ski the same day," he said. Both pursuits came naturally. He started skiing with the French Alpine Club and bagged most of the tallest summits in the area—usually with a 10-pound Komura large-format camera and a tripod in tow. He shot thousands of landscapes deep in the park that, until then, only a few mountaineers and hikers had laid eyes on. One photo from the Arête Barre Noir is his favorite, he said, taken as he straddled a knife edge with one leg of the tripod on either side. Little did he know he was documenting the end of an era.

Francou first noticed Parc des Écrins' glaciers changing in the 1980s. They had always moved, but they started moving quickly—uphill—later that decade. He flipped through his files and showed us photos of glaciers in 1985, shot again in 1998, then a few of Chautard's from the 1920s, followed by his own from 2010. The difference was dramatic. In the old pictures, the glacier is an unstoppable ice flow carving through the side of a mountain; in the new ones, it is a hanging snowfield clinging to the uppermost flanks of the mountain. The last photos he showed us were of the Noir and Blanc glaciers, the latter being the longest in the Southern Alps. In the older picture the two glaciers meet in a violent confluence. In the newer one, they languish a half mile up the valley from each other.

The issue of melting glaciers has been well-documented throughout Europe, but the speed of warming and glacial recession, especially in the south, is starting to threaten water supply and various ecosystems. The Southern Alps have always been warmer and drier than the north. Compared to data from 1961 to 1990, the average number of days with snow on the ground in the Southern Alps has decreased by two weeks, with significant melt at less than 5,000 feet.[43] Farms in the area depend heavily on Alpine glaciers for naturally stored water. With economies in southern Europe already straining the European Union's coffers, the thought of olive, grape and other regional crop yields taking a dive has EU officials watching the weather closely.

A hot debate in Europe these days is deducing exactly what is heating the continent disproportionately compared to the rest of the planet. Many point to shifting ocean and air currents—and the melting Arctic that is the engine for much of that circulation. The jet stream, which pushes weather west-east around the Northern Hemisphere, is fueled by a differential in temperature between the Arctic and warmer regions to the south. As the Arctic heats up, the relative difference decreases and the jet stream weakens and slows. The result is storms, like the one over La Grave the night before, stalling out and dropping loads of snow. Another effect is warm air from the south penetrating into the north.[44]

An influx of fresh water from melting glaciers, sea ice and ice sheets is also affecting the climate. The "thermohaline" circulation refers to deep currents of cold water that run south from the Arctic and surface currents that return warm water north. The overall effect, along with the Gulf Stream, keeps Europe warmer than it typically would be, but the rush of fresh water—which floats above salt water—seems to be disrupting the flow. While the current has slowed, scientists predict that it will remain relatively stable for the foreseeable future. If it were interrupted, it could have the opposite effect of global warming—sending mid-latitude regions like Europe and the northern U.S. into a deep freeze.[45]

Francou was one of the few climate change believers I met in the Alps. He measures snowfall on a picnic table in front of his shop and keeps a tally on the back of a card. The numbers are handwritten in pencil and, as he pointed out, have been steadily declining. Back in the day, he said, 20 feet of snow fell in town every year. Now he sees around 10.

Ptor and I drove to the grocery after Francou's. Ptor dragged a wheeled shopping basket around the brightly lit market and picked out yogurt, fruit and vegetables for his family, then a case of German beer for himself and some new lenses for his sunglasses. When researching climate change, you become hyper aware of the carbon footprint of almost every facet of modern human life: the diesel burned to deliver the beer from Germany; emissions from the Chinese factory that made Ptor's sunglasses; the electricity making the store so blindingly bright. That night at Ptor's house, we lived more sustainably, eating lamb Karin bought from a local farmer, drinking French wine by candlelight and sharing stories about another old friend who landed in La Grave: Doug Coombs.

Coombs moved to La Grave to ski, climb and teach his Steep Skiing Camps after he was banned from Jackson Hole Mountain Resort for allegedly skiing out of bounds. Ptor told me about skiing big lines with Coombs, like the incredibly steep Glacier de la Meije, Tour de la Meije and the west face of Râteau to Le Pan de Rideau. The two were neighbors in Les Terrasses and used VHF radios to communicate between their houses. When they drove to Briançon to get groceries, they'd make a pit stop to rock climb on the way home. "On the mountain, no matter what the conditions were, I would watch him ski by and think, 'If only I could ski like that,'" Ptor said. "Every turn was perfect."

Coombs died in 2006 in the Couloir de Polichinelle near La Grave. A friend and aspiring mountain guide fell off a cliff at the bottom of the steep chute, and as Coombs sidestepped down to help, his ski edge slipped. Both died as a result of their falls. Ptor had left La Grave a few years before the accident, but returned after it to mourn with friends. On that trip, he wandered into the La Chaumine and met his wife.

The moon was full when I walked to my car that night. I could see the deep-blue silhouette of La Meije across the valley and stopped for a moment to take it in. I smelled horse manure in the air and heard the trickle of the town well behind me. On the drive back to town I stopped again, this time next to Doug and Emily Coombs's old VW station wagon. It had been stored in a turnout between Ventelon and La Grave, perched on the edge of the hillside. It was white and the body was in surprisingly good shape. It glowed in the beryl light, an homage to one of the greatest skiers of all time.

The local news the next morning showed Hungarian T-72 battle tanks rolling down the highway to reach snowbound motorists. The storm had stranded thousands of people in their cars on the M1 motorway between Budapest and Vienna, many for more than a day. That morning, high winds kept the commission at La Grave from opening the resort, but the next day the gate came down and Ptor and I made our way to the gondola.

There wasn't a line or a lift attendant at the turnstile, so we walked onto the funny-looking pastel gondola cars ourselves and settled in for the ride. Giant larch trees slipped past as the cars glided uphill, and Ptor pointed out the Tabuchet and La Meije glaciers. At mid-station a gang of snowboarders loaded in, sweating, excited and covered with snow. I could see by the trenches in the slope below that there was still plenty left for us.

The top of the mountain still wasn't open, so we unloaded at the next station and Ptor skated off to skier's left. The new snow was topped with an 18-inch-thick wind slab. I stuck my pole through it and immediately felt like it could slide. Ptor waited on a giant rollover that dropped into a 35-degree slope, seemingly a perfect scenario for an avalanche. But for someone like Ptor, who has skied La Meije for decades, the conditions were just right.

He pushed off and made three signature big-mountain turns down the rollover—arms out to the side, torso perfectly still, skis a hips' width apart. I followed behind, floating on top of the creamy, wind-packed powder, then over a 10-foot "one-hitter" into a treed chute. The larches were perfectly spaced, with a few snowdrifts in between. I drifted over a column of snow-covered boulders, skied another 600 vertical feet, then hung a hard left back to the lift.

The next run, we skied the trees the whole way, turning around old-growth trunks through perfect, undisturbed powder. There is a rhythm to tree skiing where you have to match your internal cadence with openings in the forest. It is another level of communion between skier and mountain, especially when you get in a groove and let your boards run. As the old saying goes, the tree you look at is the one you're going to hit.

The powder session continued all morning in the forests of La Meije, with less than 100 other skiers there to enjoy it. The sky was bright blue and every now and then I spied the icy mass of La Meije's summit. On our last run, we leapfrogged across the flats to Chal Vachère. From there, I followed Ptor through knee-deep powder over a series of hillocks. The run dropped 1,000 vertical feet, then hooked right to the open powder fields of La Lauzette. I spotted a private chalet on the left and the

Romanche rushing through the canyon below. When I looked up, I was at eye level with town, where skiers wandered in and out of cafés and a snowplow careened down N91.

Before leaving the next day, I drove to Ptor's house to see the La Chaumine. A Belgian couple bought it recently and had renovated many of the rooms. It'd been empty since, as they were still trying to figure out how to manage it. The bar and lounge held the remains of what was once there, though: a pair of old wooden skis mounted on the wall; vintage leather boots; a canvas backpack; topo maps with routes penciled in; Fischer "Course" skis; bumper stickers from Alpine Meadows, Jackson Hole and Mad River Glen; and trophies from the Derby de la Meije—the no-rules, top-to-bottom annual race held on the mountain. Scribbled on the wall, near the bottom of a long list, was Doug Coombs's phone number.

Outside, Ptor told me about an un-skied peak he wanted to attempt in Kazakhstan. Then another, in Canada. Maybe this spring or summer, he said. We admired La Meije for a moment, then the wildflowers growing along the dirt road. He said it looked like he'd be mountain biking soon. There was a single-track trail he could ride all the way to town.

Driving down N91, I followed the water cycle again—from snow to river to power plant to conduit to the city. I stopped alongside the conduit to have a sandwich and leaned back against a cement pillar that supported a rusted-out dam gate. Upstream 50 feet, a recently installed security camera watched over an underground irrigation system that divvied up the valley's water. Glacial sediment and leaves swirled in tiny whirlpools beside me, and two mallards swam in circles downstream. Overhead, two contrails made a perfect cross, and on the highway a constant stream of cars whizzed by. When there was finally a break in the traffic, I could hear birds calling in the forest and the meditative trickle of water running downhill.

Chapter Thirteen
The Controlling Parameter

Men argue. Nature acts.

—*Voltaire*

S ix hours northeast of La Grave stands the oldest snow-science facility in the world. Before the Swiss Federal Commission for Snow and Avalanche Research (SLF) was founded in 1931, the task of mitigating and recording avalanches in Europe was left mostly to foresters, whose records described them according to their size and the devastation they wrought. Engineers built a few defensive structures to slow slides or divert them away from towns and roads, but it wasn't until winter tourism took off in Switzerland in the 1920s that officials from the ski and rail industries pushed for a more organized effort to understand the deadly phenomenon.

The Alps see more avalanches than any region in the world. In a two-month period in 1999, after heavy snow hit the area, more than 70 people were killed in slides. During WWI, avalanches—most intentionally set off by the enemy—buried 60,000 troops. Between 1941 and 1988, 7,000 avalanches were recorded in Switzerland alone, taking 1,269 lives—and giving the Swiss good cause to study the white dragon.

SLF's first sub-zero laboratory was constructed in 1935 out of snow blocks. The following winter, it was moved to a wooden shed near the summit of 8,733-foot Weissfluhjoch Mountain, where a study plot was established. Newly minted "snow scientists" developed instruments to measure things like shear strength and air permeability in a snowpack. Soon after, SLF took over the country's avalanche-warning system from the Swiss Army. Following the extreme winter of 1950–1951, when avalanches killed 98 people, the system was overhauled and SLF began collaborating with the Swiss Meteorological Office to increase forecast accuracy. That year, Ed LaChapelle arrived from the States to study and work under renowned avalanche expert André Roch.

Over the next two decades, SLF engineered avalanche barricades, planted slide-deterring forests and published guides on how explosives could safely trigger avalanches—in addition to designing the first beacons used to locate victims. In 1993 it developed a groundbreaking 2D computer model that estimated snowfall, density and morphology of the snow cover. SLF's model, called SNOWPACK, told forecasters not only how much snow would likely fall in an area and how the snowpack would evolve, but also provided the probability of a slide on certain slopes.

Around the same time, scientists started noticing a trend that few saw coming. After managing an overabundance of snow in the Alps for half a century, snow levels were diminishing. SLF has never traded in conjecture, and scientists were hesitant at first to jump on the global warming bandwagon. But when levels continued to drop, SLF scientists had little choice but to start studying why.

"The triggering event was the winter of '89 and '90," SLF climatologist Christoph Marty said. "This was a very, very low snow year, and the next winter the snow was poor as well. That, plus this whole business about climate change at the end of the '80s, let people make the connection that we might not have enough snow in the future. Though nowadays we know that winter was extremely exceptional."

Marty is SLF's head climatologist because, he said the afternoon we met in SLF's downtown Davos facility, he is its only climatologist. Marty is built like a Swiss mountaineer: broad shoulders, close-cropped brown hair, big smile and tree trunks for thighs. He smiles before he speaks and opens his eyes wide when he talks about snow. The 45-year-old grew up on the shores of Lake Zurich and learned to ski on a meadow behind his house. He skied Zermatt often with his family, but soon grew bored of trails and resorts and ventured into the backcountry. He liked the idea of choosing where he wanted to go and having to make hard decisions, like sometimes turning back. He learned that many of those choices revolved around avalanche risk, and he eventually became an intern at SLF.

Marty started full-time in 2004 and has since helped adapt SNOWPACK to make long-range forecasts for snowfall and snowpack conditions throughout Europe. The model is far more complicated, and hence prone to more errors, than one like Daniel Scott's SkiSim. But since it is physically based—on measurements taken by SLF for the last 80 years—it can be applied anywhere and provide more details, like the quality of the snow that falls.

SNOWPACK is still being developed for climatological applications, Marty said, and it gets more accurate every year. In addition to snow-cover properties, SLF scientists are adding a soil module to predict the future of permafrost—which holds many of the mountaintops in the Alps, like the Dru, together. As far as historical observation, Marty said, SLF's data reveals a clear decrease of the snowpack below 5,000 feet during the last 20 years. Altitudes above 6,500 feet, so far, see no change during the core winter season. During spring season, however, all altitudes demonstrate more intense melting.

"There was a time not so far ago that we scientists thought maybe, because warmer air can hold more humidity, climate change would bring more precipitation," he said. "And more precipitation in the higher regions would make more snow, since it was cold enough there. But nowadays from observations and also from the newest climate models, we see the temperature is really the controlling parameter, so even if we force the model with more precipitation, in the best case we can hold the current snow cover, but it will never increase. If we look at the end of the century, we see significant decrease even above 2,000 and 3,000 meters. So only the summit regions around 4,000 meters might be a little bit stable. But area-wise, that is nothing."

The overwhelming influence of temperature over precipitation has been corroborated by global and other regional models—meaning, if emissions continue to rise, snow below 13,000 feet in the Alps is living on borrowed time. On the Swiss plateau, where the majority of the country lives, there will be hardly any snow left at the end of the century. As in most regions of Europe, the snowline will climb steadily up the mountains, affecting winter tourism, agriculture, water supply and every element of Swiss life. And those forecasts assume just 3 degrees Celsius of warming by 2100.[46] If the region sees a 5 to 6 degrees Celsius rise, as many now predict, snow-covered mountains in the Alps will be a memory in three generations.

Between 60 and 80 million tourists visit the Alps every year, generating 50 billion euro in annual revenue—and 10 to 12 percent of the jobs in the region. In Austria alone, more than 250 ski resorts make up 4.5 percent of the GNP. As soon as 2030, though, the critical elevation for successful ski areas in the Alps will rise above 5,000 feet and many will have to close. For reference, Chamonix, Davos and Engelberg all have bases below 4,000 feet; Garmisch and Kitzbühel are below 3,000 feet. Austria is particularly vulnerable, where 75 percent of all ski resorts are situated below 3,200 feet. Germany is even more sensitive, losing 60 percent of snow-reliable resorts with just 1 degree Celsius of warming. On the other end of the spectrum, Switzerland will drop only 10 percent of its resorts, though higher ski areas will see the season shrink by around 50 days.[47]

Before 1990, artificial snow in the Alps was a rarity, but more resorts are turning to snowmaking to sustain their bottom lines. In Switzerland, more than 10 percent of all ski resorts use snowmaking, and in low-elevation regions of Austria and Italy, 40 percent of the ski areas need to make snow to stay viable. As in America, snowmaking is merely a stopgap—which is expensive and energy intensive. With banks and insurance companies distancing themselves from low-lying ski areas in the Alps, many resorts are having a hard time affording artificial snow. In Davos, resort officials recently pressured the community into sharing the cost of the local bus. Their latest request was for the town to chip in for snowmaking costs as well, citing a drop-off in winter visitors if lower slopes are not covered.

Europe has always been a pioneer of social and environmental progress, but many in the Alps are resistant to change. People have inhabited the Alps for more than 1,000 years and are far more familiar with natural climate fluctuations than their counterparts in America—making many in the Old World hesitant to believe that humans have anything to do with current warming. Ski areas have subsequently been forced to toe the line between preparing for the future and scaring off residents, guests and investors. In one case, reported by *The Independent* in 2004, two Swiss resorts hired consultants to analyze melting permafrost on their peaks. When the firm found that, indeed, the peaks were melting and might fall apart—taking lifts, buildings and possibly skiers with them—the resorts ordered the study stopped and the results buried.

The cold winters and deep snow of the last two years have lulled many in the Alps deeper into complacency, Marty said. Climatologists say the good winters were likely caused by unprecedented melting ice in the Barents Sea, and a resulting high-pressure system that steered Arctic air over Europe. Regardless, while governments made progress on climate change mitigation in 2012-2013, many citizens put on blinders, pointing to the snow outside their door.

"The difference between human experience and measurements is significant," Marty said. "What we nowadays think is a very good winter is true for the last 10 to 20 years, but it's nothing compared to what our measurements say it used to be in the decades before. Especially during the last five years, and especially in the Alps and some parts of northern Europe. There were some astonishing events happening with a large amount of snow. It's not what you would expect from climate change, because as a normal citizen you think linearly and you think it's getting warmer every year and so there must be less snow and so forth. But climate change is really complicated."

EU climatologists suggest the first continent-wide effects of climate change won't be felt until 2050. While average global warming is predicted to be around 2 degrees Celsius by then, warming in the Alps will likely be 3 degrees Celsius or more.[48] The hot summer of 2003—which killed 70,000 people in Europe—will become the norm. Some plant species across Europe will begin to die in the heat and, instead of absorbing carbon, will emit as much as a half-billion tons of carbon dioxide into the air as they decay.[49]

With the Greenland Ice Sheet now on track to melt out in 140 years,[50] sea-level rise will start to encroach on coastal Europe. Crops like sweet corn, grapes, sunflowers, soya and maize will shift north to regions in Britain and northern Europe. Southern countries, already tight on water, will have to alter irrigation practices as traditional crops die off.

Though 2 degrees Celsius is imperceptible to human skin, it will induce massive change to the world we know, including extinction of about a third of all species currently on the planet. Two degrees indicates the average global rise, and warming over land will be far more than over the ocean. Egypt could lose 15 percent of its wheat yield, and floods like the one in Pakistan in 2010 will become more common. In already food-scarce sub-Saharan Africa, maize and sorghum crops could decline by as much as 20 percent, and though West Africa might benefit from increased precipitation, a rapidly rising population will double food prices by mid-century.[51]

Fallout in the U.S. from a 2 degrees Celsius spike is hard to envision. Vast regions of the West and Midwest would become too hot and dry to grow food or raise livestock. The Central Valley, California's breadbasket, would lose 10 to 30 percent of its sunflower, wheat, tomato, rice, cotton and maize yields. While the northeastern United States might see 10 to 15 percent more precipitation by 2100, more intense droughts, heat waves, wildfires and floods will plague much of the rest of the country.

The effort it will take to slow global warming is almost as

staggering as its potential effects. Even if greenhouse gas emissions were stopped completely today, the planet would still heat up at least another 0.6 degrees Celsius.[52] Without major emissions reductions, PricewaterhouseCoopers's report put the chance of avoiding more than 2 degrees Celsius of warming at 50 percent, but only if nations decarbonize six times faster than they currently are. If emissions are reduced by 60 percent over the next 10 years, chances of warming less than 2 degrees Celsius rises to 93 percent.

Signs of humanity's march forward exist all around Davos. Outside town, castles cling to mountaintops above amateur ski jumps built on top of irrigation pipes that deliver glacial runoff to nearby farms. Cement factories churn out smoke on the valley floor as road crews in blaze-orange vests lay pavement on highways engineered by the Romans. On the drive to Davos I passed a self-service ski lift plopped in the middle of a village: push the button, get a ride. A few miles down the road, a man bucked logs from two fallen trees near another town that looked like it hadn't changed since the 1700s: tiled roofs, stone church, public well, goats wandering through the streets.

The first tunnels that accessed Davos were dug by hand. Now machines cut into the rock, drilling four-lane highways through the heart of the mountains. Alongside Route 28, the Glacier Express train glides over stone bridges built early in the last century on its historic route between Zermatt and St. Moritz. Some of the workers who built the line are buried just off the tracks, beneath slate tombstones set in tiny churchyards the size of a putting green.

In Davos, SLF's building on Flüelastrasse Street is a far cry from the old snow-block lab. The three-story rectangular structure is sided with solar panels. There is a display of avalanche science history in the lobby, including an array of transceivers going back 30 years. There are diagrams on the walls showing the difference between dendrite, needle, plate and hollow-column snowflakes—and charts of things like isothermal densification and metamorphism of new snow.

Hanging on the glass wall of the conference room is a relief map of the Central Alps that was published in 1907. It is stunning to see the range absent of political borders, cities or highways. Mountains on the map are a half-inch tall, separated by rivers that grow wider and deeper the farther they flow toward the sea. Great white runnels of glacial snow and ice reach down from the summits and twist through canyons. You can see the fault line that made the mountains at this scale, see the tectonic compression that pushed them up from the surface of the Earth.

A matrix of tiny red lines covers the snowfields, peaks and canyon walls. The lines represent avalanche paths, observed and recorded between 1875 and 1897. After 20 years, the map is practically all red, except for a few isolated passes and canyons. Back then it would have been hard to imagine things like computer models and X-ray microtomographic imaging technology—much less predicting when and where the devils of the high peaks would unleash their fury. Similarly, Marty said, it is difficult today to imagine a world in which there is no snow and no skiing.

"One of the things I say when people tell me, 'Oh, it doesn't matter, it's getting warmer, some people will have positive effects,' is 'Don't act for yourself, because you yourself will be gone before you see the outcome,'" he said. "But your kids will experience the end of the century. My kids will. They will be old, but definitely my grandkids will experience this. The end of the century seems to be far away now, but if you think that your grandkids will be in middle age then, that doesn't seem so far away."

Chapter Fourteen
The Carbon Count

Hell is a city much like London—a populous and a smoky city.

—*Percy Shelley, 1819*

On May 9, 2013, an observatory on Hawaii's Mauna Loa volcano, 11,135 feet above sea level, recorded the highest carbon dioxide content in the Earth's atmosphere in three million years. The milestone of 400 parts per million (ppm) was an average for the day. The last time carbon dioxide levels were that high, horses and giant camels roamed the swamplands of the Arctic. Back then, the world was cooling off from an epic greenhouse warming period. Now, it is heading into one.

The atmosphere contained around 180 ppm of carbon dioxide during the last Ice Age. Warmer interglacial periods measured about 280 ppm. The 400 ppm count was a milestone not only because it almost doubled pre–Industrial Revolution levels, but also because it symbolized the failure of humanity to deal with the mess it started two and a half centuries ago. If current trends continue, carbon dioxide emissions are expected to jump another 20 percent by 2020.

The measurement on Mauna Loa didn't last long. Carbon dioxide levels are highest in May before springtime blossoms and leaves draw the gas out of the air. Two days after it was announced, NOAA reduced the original May 9 count to 399.89 due to a discrepancy, and conservative pundits cried foul. Eleven-hundredths of a point is no cause for uproar. In fact, 350 ppm is the number people should keep in mind when debating climate change mitigation, says one of the world's leading environmentalists, Bill McKibben. "In 20 years, at our current pace, we'll breeze past 450 ppm of carbon dioxide in the atmosphere," he says. "At 400, we've melted the Arctic; it will be interesting to see what large physical features of the planet we manage to break in the next two decades."

McKibben's sarcasm is closer to reality. He has been in the green game full-time since the 1980s and has seen climate change warnings answered by emissions rising instead of falling. He moved north to the Adirondack Mountains after quitting a job at *The New Yorker* as a staff writer to write books about climate change, human behavior, population growth and training for elite endurance events. He has published a dozen books since then and become one of the leading activists advocating for climate change mitigation. In 2006 he organized a walk across Vermont to protest a lack of climate change legislation; then, in 2007, he initiated the "Step It Up" campaign to push Congress to mandate an 80 percent reduction in greenhouse gases by 2050. In 2009 he founded 350.org with seven graduate students at Middlebury College, where he teaches—and on October 24, 2009, the group orchestrated the "most widespread day of political action" in history, with 5,245 events in 181 countries.

The threshold of 350 ppm comes from a talk James Hansen gave while he was heading NASA's Goddard Institute for Space Studies. Three hundred fifty is the tipping point, Hansen said, "if humanity wishes to preserve a planet similar to that on which civilization developed and to which life on Earth is adapted." So recent talk about passing 400 ppm and life in a 4 degrees Celsius warmer world is a continuum, McKibben says. We have already gone too far, and if we keep debating and not acting, we'll pass 2 degrees Celsius and lose control of the thermostat.

McKibben's most recent campaigns target the source of the problem. *Do the Math*, a documentary film, spells out exactly how, when and why taking carbon out of the earth and putting it into the sky will destroy human civilization. The math, as McKibben explains in the movie, is simple: to keep warming below the 2 degrees Celsius threshold, the world can emit no more than 565 gigatons of additional carbon dioxide into the air. The problem is, fossil fuel companies like Exxon, Chevron, BP, Shell and ConocoPhillips now have the equivalent of 2,795 giga tons of carbon dioxide in their reserves—enough to burn up the world five times over—and they don't have any intention of leaving it there.[53]

"Getting a real international agreement—or, for that matter, action by Congress—will require breaking the power of the fossil fuel industry to block action," McKibben says. "Since they're the richest industry in history, that won't be easy—but it's why we're busy building a movement, working on divestment, going to jail and highlighting the very real alternatives."

In 2011, the top five oil companies made a combined profit of $375 million a day. From that income, they spent an average of $440,000 a day lobbying Congress and received $6.6 million a day in federal tax breaks—all while remaining the only industry in the world that is not taxed for its waste. Exxon's CEO, Rex Tillerson, clears $100,000 a day himself, and even admitted in 2012 that anthropogenic climate change is happening. "I'm not disputing that increasing CO_2 emissions in the atmosphere is going to have an impact. It'll have a warming impact," he said. He then went on to accuse "lazy journalists" and an "illiterate public" of blowing the problem out of proportion. (Exxon spent $223,000 on Tillerson's personal security in 2012.)

Another set of numbers McKibben points out is equally alarming. Every year, 30 billion tons of carbon dioxide is released, and every year, that number grows by about three percent. So in 15 years the limit of 565 gigatons will be exceeded. The 2013 IPCC report recognized the limit for the first time, but extended the deadline to 2040. Either way, the timing is too tight to wait any longer, McKibben says, so he has gone on the offensive to force change. "Go Fossil Free" is a divestment initiative to get colleges, governments, institutions and individuals to liquidate investment in 200 publicly traded companies that hold most of the world's coal, oil and gas reserves. The movement is similar to one that thousands of students used in the 1990s to convince colleges to divest from corporations connected to South Africa during apartheid. Already, "Go Fossil Free" has spread to more than 300 college campuses across the U.S.

The goals of the campaign are multifold. The first is to force oil companies to shift to renewable resources. The second is to reveal what McKibben says are the true rogues in society—whose businesses are inexorably destroying the Earth and killing hundreds of thousands of people a year—and get them to pledge to keep 80 percent of their current reserves underground forever. If they don't, "they should lose their social license," he says, "their veneer of respectability."

Rich nations repeatedly point a finger at developing countries like China and India when it comes to emissions. If you look at the last two centuries, though, the U.S. is to blame for most of the world's aggregate carbon problem, followed closely by Germany and the U.K. All three countries still have some of the highest per capita carbon footprints in the world. The U.S. represents five percent of the world's population, but it contributes a quarter of its carbon dioxide. Germany and the U.K. are high on the list as well, with 10.4 and 9.7 million metric tons of carbon emissions, per capita respectively, between 1980 and 2006.[54]

A little less than half of the carbon dioxide in the atmosphere stays there for around 150 years after it is released. The rest can remain for thousands.[55] Much of the oldest emissions in the air today were created by factories in the 1860s making cannons for the American Civil War—and British engineers finishing the first leg of the London Underground. Governments and big business take the brunt of the blame for the rising carbon count, but almost all emissions can be traced back to consumers, in either direct or indirect ways. In the U.S. in 2003, direct household operations like heating and refrigeration created an average of 12 tons of carbon dioxide per house per year. An equal amount came from personal automobiles. Indirect causes—like shipping, lighting and air conditioning in businesses that consumers frequent—added another 35 tons. Total household emissions in the U.S. are now six times more than the global average.

China is quickly closing the carbon gap. It passed the U.S. in 2007 as the largest producer of carbon dioxide. In the next eight years the Chinese will build 800,000 megawatts of new coal-fired power plants—two and a half times the total number of plants currently installed in the U.S. Projections suggest that China will emit the same amount of carbon dioxide between 2000 and 2030 as the U.S. did during the entire 20th century.[56]

Profits have precluded most environmental concerns in China until now, but after massive protests against air pollution, the State Council made concessions. Air quality in Beijing in January 2013 hit a level of toxicity 40 times above the World Health Organization's safety threshold. China's blogs logged 2.5 million posts mentioning smog that month, and activists held rallies across the country. Official response at first was to jail environmental activists and mandate a state-approved body as a gatekeeper for all environmental lawsuits. But in April the government announced a bilateral climate change working group with the U.S., and later the two countries signed a deal to reduce emissions and fund carbon-capture technology.

After the Chinese government committed to spending $275 billion over the next five years to clean up air pollution—and initiated a progressive cap-and-trade program in seven cities—it seemed the country was getting on board with mitigation. One motive analysts pointed out: most of China sits at sea level.

Air quality in London in the mid-19th century was not so different from Beijing in 2013. The word "smog" was born in London in the early 1900s to describe the suffocating mix of fog and smoke in the city. Before the Industrial Revolution, wind and water powered most of England, but after, coal was the fuel of choice. Air pollution became so bad, a recent study by Austrian researchers found that soot settling on Alpine glaciers—subsequently darkening and melting them—likely helped bring an early end to the Little Ice Age.[57]

The exodus to high ground and clean air in the mountains in the 1800s was a boon to hotels in the Alps. England was the fastest-industrializing country in Europe and subsequently had the most pollution, money and travelers. In 1865, a third of the 11,789 tourists who passed through Chamonix were British, giving the valley the moniker "Little London of the High Alps."[58] In kind, a majority of the alpinists who made history climbing in the range claimed peaks with a Union Jack.

Like Pococke and Windham in the 1700s, 19th century climbers were typically wealthy gentlemen. Some continued the scientific experiments of their forbearers, carrying barometers and boiling-point thermometers to estimate things like relative humidity, solar radiation, the composition of the air and the air's "transparency." Increasingly, though, expeditions became more about sport, and with that came fierce competition.

Some important ascents during the Golden Age of Alpinism included the Eiger in 1858, by Charles Barrington, and the Dom, summited the same year by J. L. Davies. In 1861 a prominent scientist from Ireland set out to climb the 14,783-foot Weisshorn in southwest Switzerland. John Tyndall started the ascent from the small town of Randa with two guides at 1:00 p.m. The group bivouacked that night and made good progress in the morning, until they found themselves stuck on an icy knife-edge ridge with a dangerous drop-off on either side. "I thought of Englishmen in battle, of the qualities which had made them famous: it was mainly the quality of not knowing when to yield—of fighting for duty even after they had ceased to be animated by hope," Tyndall wrote of the four-hour slog up the final pitch. The group eventually made it to the summit and, 11 hours later, returned to Randa to tell the tale.

Tyndall was one of the few alpinists who was a successful scientist before he was a climber. He loved the thin air and open spaces of the mountains and returned every summer after his first visit in 1856, mapping and analyzing glacial mechanics and the flow of tributaries that feed the Mer de Glace. At home, he studied radiant energy and the energy-absorbing qualities of certain gases. In the late 1850s he invented a tool to measure absorption of solar radiation in the atmosphere—and became the first to prove the basic principles of the greenhouse effect.

Scientists Joseph Fourier and Claude Pouillet first discovered the greenhouse effect in the 1820s. They were trying to figure out why the Earth didn't burn up from the sun's heat, or freeze at night, and realized that, like a glass covering a box, the atmosphere trapped some of the sun's warmth. Tyndall found that water vapor was the greatest insulator, without which, he said, "The warmth of our fields and gardens would pour itself unrequited into space, and the sun would rise upon an island held fast in the grip of frost." The next was carbon dioxide.

There is a certain irony to the fact that many of the first expeditions onto the high glaciers of the Alps were directly or indirectly funded by factories belching smoke that would ultimately doom the ice. Not that anyone, including Tyndall, foresaw it at the time. In fact, it took more than a century in Europe before the first rumblings of global warming made their way to the national stage.

The 1972 Stockholm Conference kicked off the modern era of environmental policy in Europe, even though the debate over whether the planet was warming or cooling was still being waged. Since then, the European Union has pioneered the renewable-energy market, emissions reduction, industrial sustainability and climate policy. In 2005 the EU was one of the few entities to follow through on its commitment in Kyoto to reduce greenhouse gases to seven percent below 1990 levels. By 2011, emissions were 17.5 percent below the benchmark level. Even with recent economic setbacks, the EU says it is on track to make its ambitious 20-20-20 goal: 20 percent emissions reduction below 1990 levels, 20 percent increase in renewable energy and 20 percent reduction of overall energy consumption.

The EU's 2005 cap-and-trade scheme has been a model throughout the world for how to mitigate climate change without devastating the economy. The Emissions Trading Scheme "cap" denotes a limit on total emissions that gets tighter over time. The "trade" refers to pollution permits that companies are allotted by the government that they can barter. Between 2005 and 2010, the scheme cut emissions to affected sectors by 13 percent while the GDP grew slightly—effectively severing the long-held association between economic growth and emissions. The plan wasn't perfect, and after initially handing out too many permits, carbon prices fell dramatically. Critics also claimed that the economic slowdown in the EU was partially responsible for emissions reductions.

As in the U.S., changes in the weather helped push recent legislation in Europe. Between 1980 and 2007, 1,097 climate-related disasters[59] rocked the continent, including the deadly heat wave of 2003 and scores of floods, droughts and even blizzards. Almost three-quarters of Europeans live in cities, making them highly susceptible to natural disasters. And as the continent heats up, policy makers are wondering what will happen if mitigation doesn't happen quickly enough. As the World Bank's report *Turn Down the Heat* points out, even if all international carbon-reduction pledges are carried out, "the world [is] on a trajectory for a global mean warming of well over 3 degrees Celsius." Even more alarming, there is a 50 percent chance in that scenario that temperatures rise 5 degrees Celsius and a 25 percent chance they go to 6 degrees Celsius.

In terms of snow, almost all of the experts I spoke with in the Alps assumed a 2 to 4 degrees Celsius warming scenario—meaning the situation might be worse than current predictions. The close of *Turn Down the Heat* sums up the situation best: "Given that it remains uncertain whether adaptation and further progress toward development goals will be possible at this level of climate change, the projected 4 degrees Celsius warming simply must not be allowed to occur—the heat must be turned down. Only early, cooperative, international actions can make that happen."[60]

Chapter Fifteen

Energiewende

Nothing is impossible. You are only limited by fear and even that you can overcome.

—*Seth Morrison*

T he bridge that crosses the Inn River in western Austria has been a prize for European powers since Roman times. Back then, Brenner Pass, due south, was the primary link between Italy and the northern Roman province of Raetia. The pass is the lowest of the major passages through the Alps and was used by the Alamanni, the Counts of Tyrol and Emperor Frederick Barbarossa on his campaigns into Italy.

To cross the Inn Valley you have to cross the river—hence the name Innsbruck, meaning "bridge over the Inn." Innsbruck was once the capital of Tyrol and the home of Hapsburg emperors and archdukes. It was ceded to Bavaria by Napoleon, then annexed by Austria in 1918. In 1938 Austria joined Germany's Third Reich and the Allies bombed Innsbruck, targeting the convergence of four major rail lines that supplied the Italian front.

Allied sorties spared a few relics of the city's past, like the green tower of the Hofkirche church, built in 1553 and visible as you funnel into the tiny, circular roads of downtown. It had been snowing for two days when I arrived, and tiny flakes sifted over the eaves of the imperial court and multicolored row houses stacked alongside the river. I followed the glacial-blue Inn through town, then hung a left on Weiherburggasse Street, a serpentine alley that leads to the office of one of the Alps' leading climatologists.

Innsbruck University's Management Center (MCI) has been around since 1995, offering bachelor and graduate degrees in "management and society, technology and life sciences." Dr. Robert Steiger joined the staff in 2012 as a teacher and researcher. He met me in the lobby, hand outstretched. It was Easter Break. "Only for the students," Steiger laughed, his voice echoing through the empty hallways. Steiger became interested in climate change when he drove by a ski area in Bavaria one spring and saw only a few lifts still open. He wondered how long ski areas could survive in a warmer world and if his kids would be able to ski the same places he did.

Steiger has the lanky build of a basketball player and reddish-brown hair that he parts to the side. He grew up near Munich and used to drive for hours on winter weekends to ski with his family. Since he moved to Innsbruck, he skis with his wife and two children practically outside his back door. With nine ski areas circling downtown, Innsbruck is one of the greatest skiing cities in the world. Many of them, like the vertical slopes and chutes of Nordpark and the wide-open runs at Patscherkofel, can be accessed directly from the city.

When he is not on the hill, Steiger works with Daniel Scott and the SkiSim model. He added a refined snowmaking module to the model and applied it to Tyrol and South Tyrol. In February 2013 he and Johann Stötter published the paper "Climate Change Impact Assessment of Ski Tourism in Tyrol." The paper looked at 111 ski areas in Austria and Italy and found that all would require 100 percent snowmaking coverage to maintain snow reliability through the 2030s and 2040s—and that even then, Christmas snow reliability would be questionable by the 2020s.[61] Steiger listed off a few ski hills that had already closed when we spoke— Gschwender Horn, Immenstadt, Tarscher Alm, Latsch, Kufstein, Fürstalm and Kramsach, the last of which sits just 25 miles outside of Innsbruck. If the temperature rises 3 degrees Celsius, most of the areas in the study would likely have to close.

Steiger's predictions for high-altitude snow elsewhere in the Alps were somewhat more optimistic. Climate change varies greatly throughout the Alps, he said, with some areas able to withstand only a half-degree of change and others able to weather change of up to 4 degrees Celsius. "The scenarios we use for the Alps say they will warm 2 degrees Celsius by 2050 and up to 4 degrees Celsius by 2100," he said. "The most sensitive ski areas are typically along the Northern Alps at lower altitudes. The least sensitive ski areas are in Switzerland, above 2,000 meters or more. Even in a 2 or 3 degrees Celsius future, they probably won't have a problem in the next 50 to 100 years—maybe in some parts of the ski area in the valley, but not high up."

A lack of high-emissions models in the Alps is a setback when it comes to accurately predicting snow cover above 4 degrees Celsius, Steiger said. Another impediment to mitigating climate change that has bothered him recently is a new buzzword spreading across the continent. "Adaptation" refers to changes in infrastructures, economies and lifestyles to prepare for what many see as an inevitably warmer future. To many scientists and environmentalists in Europe, the approach sends the wrong message: that there's nothing humans can do to slow global warming.

The EU launched its adaptation strategy in the spring of 2013 with the intention of "anticipating the adverse effects of climate change and taking appropriate action to prevent or minimize the damage they can cause." Some adaptation strategies include creating reservoirs to replace the water storage that glaciers offer, making buildings more resistant to extreme weather events, building up dikes, creating corridors for migrating animals and even finding sports that could replace skiing in the Alps.

Steiger knows adaptation theory well. Before he started at MCI, he worked for the AlpS Centre for Climate Change Adaptation Technologies, helping companies and industries strategize for a warming climate. While some preparation is necessary, widespread restructuring ultimately signals that people are giving up. It also diverts money and attention away from a far more important goal. "Unfortunately they're not talking so much about mitigation anymore," he said. "We talk a lot about adaptation, but actually we could solve the problems that occur at the moment. Adaptation is not securing the future or the future of our children."

There's a paradox in asking European ski areas to spend millions of dollars to transition to renewable energy—much less find the loans to do it with—when there's a good chance they could go out of business in the near future. What Steiger found in the winter tourism sector was that most executives understood and believed in climate change, but short of closing down the ski resort, they felt there was nothing they could do. Because ski areas in Europe are typically owned by several entities—one runs the lifts, another the restaurants, another the hotels—creating a unified voice like resorts in America have is difficult.

Groups like the Ski Club of Great Britain's "Respect the Mountains" represent the few that are raising awareness of climate change and its effect on snow. Web sites like "Snowcarbon" and "Save Our Snow" give helpful tips to European skiers on how to reduce their carbon footprint, but there are no organizations like Protect Our Winters lobbying politicians and affecting widespread change. Large-scale efforts like the International Commission for the Protection of the Alps and the Alpine Convention have to navigate eight governments, a half dozen languages and vastly different cultures and populations—and have become bogged down in bureaucracy as a result.

Until resorts get onboard, Steiger said, skiers can make a difference. The first step: change the way they move. Fifty million cars drive through the Alps every year. If people want to take control of mitigation, they can get a head start by walking or riding bicycles short distances instead of getting into a car, or carpool to reduce the number of vehicles on the road. Buildings account for 40 percent of global greenhouse gas emissions and are another area where citizens can make a difference. Using more efficient lighting could save enough electricity to close 705 of the world's 2,800 coal-fired power plants.[62] Even simple things like painting a roof white to reflect the sun's heat reduces cooling costs and limits carbon dioxide emissions. In fact, painting all of the roofs in the world white would be the equivalent of taking 24 billion tons of carbon dioxide out of the atmosphere. The strategy is simple, Steiger says, but convincing people to do it is another matter.

"The hardest thing about mitigation is behavioral change—using less energy in the household for warming, for cooling," he said. "They say the first 10 to 20 percent of any energy reduction is quite easy to achieve. Just to try to walk to the supermarket, for example—actually a small thing. But after the 10 to 20 percent, there is a need to change your behavior. And that's hard for people to think about. Because it seems less comfortable if you have to take your bike or if you have to walk. If you're not allowed to go on holiday to the Seychelles or the Caribbean from Europe. You want to do what you want, so your freedom is very much combined with mobility."

The end result is a kind of stasis. A few Alpine ski areas are trying to introduce geothermal, hydro- and solar power, but on a limited scale that won't move the needle. With little else to do, many resorts are installing snowmaking that will make their slopes white while consuming more energy. The only way forward, Steiger said, is to get beyond the fear of climate change and address it head on.

"Climate change is always seen as something very frightening or something very dangerous; you don't want to talk about it," he said. "Some people think we have to change everything within a year or two or so. Within the tourism sector I would say we have about one generation to react. It takes about 10 or 20 years when one generation comes to the position of deciding what to do. We are still lucky that we have that time to react, to adapt to climate change, but what we should think about is to mitigate it."

The generation my parents grew up in saw more social change than most: civil rights, women's rights, Vietnam, the environmental movement. My mother was 19 years old on January 25, 1966, when she exercised her own personal liberty and boarded an Icelandic Air jet bound for Munich. She didn't have much money. She didn't have permission from her parents. She had just gone through a painful breakup with a longtime boyfriend. All she knew was that she wanted to get far away from that and her job in New York City and ski.

She arrived in St. Anton, Austria—60 miles west of Innsbruck—three days after leaving the States and found a room in a family-run Bavarian *pensione* called the Haus Lina. Every morning the older couple who owned it served her an egg, salami, cheese and bread. She enrolled in the Ski School Arlberg, which Austrian ski star Hannes Schneider founded in 1921, and explored the slopes of St. Anton, Lech and Zürs. In the afternoons she lounged on the porch of the Hotel Post, Krazy Kanguruh bar or the Bahnhof, where food and wine were cheap and young people from all over the world mingled. Europe was booming again after rebuilding from the war, and—just two years before the Paris student uprisings and the Prague Spring—*joie de vivre i*n the streets and on the slopes buzzed.

I grew up with photos of that winter, and subsequent others, papering the walls of our bathroom—black-and-white images framed in Plexiglas and strips of white pine. In the pictures, my parents have long hair and dark tans. They are either sitting in shadowy restaurants or skiing through white aprons of snow. It was strange to see a ski slope with no trees on it. The mountains I learned on had nothing *but* trees. The place in the pictures was exotic, and in my mind I swore that one day I would be there.

More than most sports, skiing is handed down through the generations. It doesn't always stick, but when it does, it often sticks for life. My grandfather taught his family to ski. He was a lifetime outdoorsman and gave ski lessons on hay that he spread across the steep backyard of their house in Philadelphia. In the winter the family road-tripped to the Poconos and Vermont to ski the icy slopes of the East. When he had time to board a plane, the Alps were his favorite getaway.

My grandfather skied all over Europe with my grandmother, schussing down the glaciers of France, Austria and Switzerland and squeezing his six-foot-two frame into tiny chalet hotel rooms. He was awarded a bronze star in the Battle of the Bulge during World War II and had a special place in his heart for the old country. The only war stories that he told were of valor, humor and the shenanigans of fellow soldiers. Many of his peers were drafted, but others, like my grandfather, volunteered. The understanding in America at the time was that a great evil was spreading around the globe. Hitler had taken over almost all of Europe by the time my grandfather arrived at the front. It was the last great global crisis that engulfed the planet. That is, until now.

Sixteen is the magic number in the current battle. That's how many terawatts (one trillion watts) it takes to power humanity for a day. With 173,000 terawatts of solar energy hitting the planet continuously, 870 terawatts blowing in the wind and 32 terawatts of geothermal energy bubbling close to the surface of the earth, burning fossil fuels starts to look ludicrous. Renewable energy now accounts for two terawatts of global consumption. Most experts agree that world leaders have a few decades to make it to 16. They are also very clear that it's not going to be easy. To get another two terawatts of wind power in the U.S. alone, the country would have to build one turbine every five minutes for the next 25 years.

Mitigation advocates often make an analogy between the effort needed to stop global warming and the mobilization it took to defeat Hitler. In his State of the Union address in 1942, FDR proposed that the U.S. produce 45,000 tanks, 60,000 planes, 20,000 anti-aircraft guns and several thousand ships in a matter of years to win the war. It was an impossible task, unprecedented and mocked by many. As it turned out, the critics were correct. It didn't take years. All of FDR's goals were met in a matter of months.

You have to be creative to achieve the impossible. FDR banned private-car production, road construction and recreational driving. Tires, gasoline, fuel oil and sugar were rationed. A company making sparkplugs was retooled to turn out machine guns. A merry-go-round factory produced gun mounts, and a toy company churned out compasses. Grenade belts were stitched by a corset manufacturer, and armor-piercing shells were left to a plant that once made pinballs. As England's Foreign Secretary, Sir Edward Grey, famously said, "The United States is like a giant boiler. Once the fire is lighted under it, there is no limit to the power it can generate."

The amount of renewable power that the world needs to generate in the next 30 years is daunting. Building a turbine every five minutes might seem impossible, yet at its peak GM built six cars every minute. Germany's controversial Energiewende (Energy Transformation) program is on track to make an 80 percent reduction of greenhouse gas emissions by 2050, while decommissioning all nuclear power plants in the country. Japan has pledged to reduce emissions by 25 percent below 1990 levels by 2020, and Brazil is aiming to reach 1994 levels—in addition to reducing deforestation by 80 percent—in the same timeframe. Unfortunately, in the U.S., even with Obama's Climate Action Plan, the meager goal of a 17 percent reduction by 2020 doesn't look probable.

Population growth is predicted to swell energy demand by 56 percent between 2010 and 2040, making the effort to cut emissions even harder. But with nearly $90 billion in subsidies for renewable energy industries around the world, creative solutions are coming online. The 1.2-megawatt SeaGen tidal power plant makes electricity from two turbines that spin as the tide rushes in and out near Strangford Lough, Ireland. The 240-megawatt Alholmens Kraft biofuel power plant in Pietarsaari, Finland, is powered by locally sourced bark, branches and peat—as are portable biomass generators made by All Power Labs in San Francisco. Projects like the Aguçadoura Wave Farm near Póvoa de Varzim, Portugal, which uses wave motion to turn turbines, will help renewable energy likely surpass natural gas as the second largest source of electricity, after coal, by 2016.

There are myriad challenges in the world, like cancer and aging, that humans haven't figured out how to solve. It's surprising that the one we have a solution for—and that happens to be the largest threat to our race in history—is the one most people are hesitant to tackle. As FDR said in his inaugural address in 1933 in the depths of the Great Depression, fear is indeed the silent enemy:

> This is preeminently the time to speak the truth, the whole truth, frankly and boldly. Nor need we shrink from honestly

facing conditions in our country today. This great Nation will endure as it has endured, will revive and will prosper. So, first of all, let me assert my firm belief that the only thing we have to fear is fear itself—nameless, unreasoning, unjustified terror which paralyzes needed efforts to convert retreat into advance.

Chapter Sixteen
The Age of Humans

He blinked at the sun and dreamt that perhaps he might snare it and spare it as it went down to its resting place amidst the distant hills.

—*H. G. Wells*

After running one of the most successful companies in the world and serving as the 16th U.S. ambassador to the Soviet Union, Tom Watson Jr. decided there was one more mountain he needed to climb. The second president of IBM—his father was the first—kept a checklist on his desk of adventures he wanted to undertake when he retired. Climbing the Matterhorn was near the top, so when he arrived at the mountain's base in the little farming village of Zermatt in 1983, he tracked down one of the best guides in the valley to lead the way.

Paul Julen was already a legend by then. Julen grew up in the 1940s with 12 brothers and sisters on a small farm above town. His family had no money. His father sold a sheep or a goat in the fall and the Julens survived on the money until spring. Julen couldn't afford pencils, so he brought burned matches to write with at the tiny schoolhouse in town. One day a man took his father aside and said, "Every child you have, the community will have to pay for someday."

Julen took a job as a carpenter soon after. He went to work before the sun rose and to bed not long after getting home. Zermatt was exploding as a popular ski destination then and Julen's brothers learned to ski, race and eventually teach. Julen noticed that they were asleep when he went to the shop in the morning and relaxing on the deck when he got home—and that they made 10 times more money than him. So he walked to town, bought his first pair of skis and hit the slopes. A few years later when he took the Swiss ski-instructor certification test, he showed his examiners a relaxed new style of skiing that he'd invented. It flew in the face of the rigid Arlberg technique of the time. Julen said he wanted to teach it to students, and the examiners laughed, gave him a passing grade and mockingly wished him luck. Two years later, Julen enrolled 2,000 students in his clinic and had to drive to Verbier to find more instructors.

Julen flapped his arms and swung his head around in the lobby of the Hotel Matterhornblick to demonstrate his technique. He looked more like a flamingo trying to get something off its back than a ski instructor, but his description sounded familiar. "Forget all zee rules!" he chirped. "Let your body do what it was meant to do!" Kind of like a freeskier—in the 1950s.

It was warm the day we met in downtown Zermatt, with thick clouds capping the valley. I'd arrived from Innsbruck the day before. Julen told a half dozen stories that started with something like "A priest, a rabbi and a carpenter walk into a bar..." and ended with him shrugging his shoulders as if to say, "What can you do?" Which is exactly how his favorite story, the one of Tom Watson Jr. trying to climb the Matterhorn, went.

Julen was still moonlighting as a carpenter, in addition to teaching skiing and guiding climbers, when Watson arrived. Locals were so proficient by then on the standard Hornli Ridge route, where bolts and guidelines are permanently installed, that they said they could lead a cow up the 14,690-foot hook-nosed peak. It wasn't always that way. When Edward Whymper first climbed the mountain in 1865, it had already repelled dozens of expeditions from France, Switzerland and Italy. On the way down from their successful bid, Whymper's expedition lost four members when a rope broke.

Julen sent Watson to the Hörnlihütte—the last refuge where climbers can sleep before the final push up the mountain. When Julen arrived that night, he found Watson supine in his bunk, gazing at his watch and taking his pulse. He told Julen that he didn't care what happened to him after he reached the summit; he just needed to get there no matter what.

They set out at 11:00 p.m., four hours before the other climbers in the hut, and made slow progress. Watson was 69 years old at the time and not in terribly good shape. By dawn they were within sight of the top. Watson had slowed considerably, but the pair persevered and by mid-morning they made the summit. Watson was jubilant, but unsure he could get back down. Julen spotted a helicopter flying by and told Watson to lie on his back. His client did as he was told and Julen signaled to the pilot that there was an emergency. A rope was dropped and Julen secured it around Watson's chest. Because of the thin air, and Watson's impressive mass, the pilot couldn't lift him. So Julen signaled for the chopper to fly over the sheer southeast face—where he could descend to thicker air with Watson dangling below. The pilot understood and hovered above the precipice. Julen double-checked his knots, then bid farewell to the man *Fortune* magazine once called "the greatest capitalist in history" and pushed him off the top of the Matterhorn.

A triumphant Watson landed in town minutes later and another story was added to Zermatt's canon—a saga that recounts the evolution of a feudal farming hamlet into the most exclusive ski resort in the world. Zermatt has been a crossroads since the Romans conquered Valais and created a vast network of roads connecting to Theodul Pass. (A T-bar runs over the pass now.) From there the village followed the path of many in Valais. The region was slowly Germanized, and small hamlets like Blatten, Furi and Zum See were formed. Most of the farmers raised cattle and lived in wooden chalets, with barns raised off the earth by pillars and flat stone disks to keep vermin out. As tourism and alpinism spread throughout the Alps, farmers became mountain guides and houses were converted into hotels.

More than three dozen 4,000-meter peaks encircle Zermatt, and the area was one of the world's earliest alpine centers. The Klein Matterhorn was first climbed in 1792, just six years after the conquest of Mont Blanc. The first 4,000-meter peak in the valley to be summited was the Breithorn, on August 13, 1813. Skis didn't show up until 1898, when two Germans, Wilhelm Paulcke and Robert Helbling, became the first people to ascend with skis above 4,000 meters. That winter, the pair sent Norwegian skis to the villagers who'd helped them, and the slopes around the valley have been tracked ever since.

Zermatt didn't get on the commercial skiing train until relatively late in the game. Skiers hiked or rode the Gornergrat train until the first lift was installed in 1942. Two years later there were more winter visitors than summer, and by the winter of 1946, 70,000 guests spent the night. These days, two million people visit the town every year and there are more than 130 hotels crammed into the valley, 40 of which are rated four-star. The day after Christmas the population surges from 6,000 to 40,000, most of whom come to ski 150 miles of trails over more than 7,000 vertical feet at the resort—including terrain accessed by the Klein Matterhorn tram, the tallest lift in Europe.

The explosion made local landowners like Paul Julen millionaires, but it has come at a cost to the local environment. Electric buses have been the primary means of transportation since the 1940s because air pollution in the narrow valley blocked the view of the Matterhorn. Many buildings are still heated by oil and don't comply with modern energy standards. More than a dozen large construction projects start every year, even though the village is literally running out of space. Recently the town had to build a new wastewater treatment center, rated for 65,000 people—more than 10 times the number of actual residents.

The Swiss are efficient above all things, so it was strange to see diesel exhaust belching from a giant bulldozer my first day in town. Officials say they have cut Zermatt's greenhouse gas emissions in half in recent years. A new youth hostel is the first in town to comply with stringent new energy codes, and a new luxury hotel bored holes into the ground beneath it to heat the building with geothermal energy. Zermatt Mountain Cableways, which runs the resort's lifts, has optimized snowmaking efforts and installed solar panels at the Trockener Steg cable-car station and the

Matterhorn Glacier Paradise station, which also uses wastewater to make snow. But the efforts are window dressing when it comes to slowing global warming.

Low-elevation ski areas around the Bernese Oberland will see the effects of climate change far sooner than higher ones around Graubünden and Valais.[63] Still, ski areas like Zermatt are already preparing for a warmer future. Glacial melt has left a sizable gap between the Trockener Steg lift station and the Theodul Glacier, home of Zermatt's popular summer skiing slopes. Zermatt Mountain Cableways spends $4 million a year filling it in with an advanced snowmaking system that operates above freezing. The resort is also expanding warm-weather activities in the event that the mountain melts out faster than expected. One silver lining of climate change for mountain resorts: hotels have seen increased summer bookings by tourists who say the Mediterranean is getting too hot.

The ebb and flow of Zermatt's glaciers has been a constant throughout history. During Roman occupation, glaciers like the Findelen grew substantially, prohibiting travel over nearby passes. Four hundred years later, glaciers receded and roads over the passes reopened. Larch forests sprung up where there once was ice, until the glaciers advanced again and mowed them down. When glacial ice peaked in 1850, it knocked over farmhouses and covered valuable grazing pastures.

The most recent melt, Paul Julen said, is part of the cycle. Julen remembered stories of panicked farmers selling off their land in the 1800s, only to see it uncovered again decades later. "What are you going to do?" he laughed, shrugging his shoulders. Until it gets cold again, snowmaking, water rationing and adaptation will bridge the gap. "It's what we've always done," he said.

IBM has always been ahead of its time. The company was an early adopter of energy conservation, tracking consumption as early as 1973. An efficiency initiative between 1990 and 2012 saved an estimated 6.1 billion kilowatt-hours of electricity. Since then, IBM has invested in climate change modeling in South Africa and solar panel research. Its "Water for Tomorrow" project, in collaboration with The Nature Conservancy, also helps develop forecasting tools to better manage the world's rivers.

It's another computer pioneer, though, who is funding what people in the climate change world call "Plan B"—the last resort if reducing emissions doesn't work. Bill Gates entered the global warming arena the way he embarks on any large project: by hiring top experts in the field to teach him in his living room. Gates's interest lies in an area of study called geoengineering—defined as a deliberate, large-scale intervention into the Earth's systems to control global warming. The science has vacillated somewhere between science fiction and experimentation since the 1960s. Proposals include igniting a nuclear weapon on the moon to make its orbit shade the Earth from sunlight and planting mechanical trees with chemically coated leaves that draw carbon dioxide out of the air.

Gates has invested millions into researching schemes like stretching hoses, suspended by balloons, into the stratosphere to spray sulfates that reflect solar radiation—and building machines to churn the ocean in the paths of hurricanes to weaken them.[64] One project on which he collaborated with NASA designed ships that could spray seawater 3,000 vertical feet into clouds and make them more reflective.

The most obvious way to slow warming is to take carbon dioxide out of the air. Carbon capture and sequestration gained traction in 2007 when Sir Richard Branson and Al Gore announced a $25 million prize for anyone who could remove a billion tons of carbon dioxide from the atmosphere every year for a decade. No one has claimed the prize, but several companies are in the running. Most use sorbents that bind to carbon dioxide, then release it in another process. The scheme would require thousands of tall, narrow structures that filter air through honeycomb-like capturing chambers. No company has perfected a product yet, but several demo units have been made. Global Thermostat recently finished a sample plant that captures around two tons of carbon dioxide a day.

The biggest hurdle to capturing carbon has been making the machines profitable. One of the greatest ironies of climate change is that there is a competitive market for carbon dioxide. Companies that make dry ice, carbonated drinks and plant food currently pay around $100 a ton for the gas. The greatest of all the great ironies is that the oil industry is the biggest potential customer. It uses carbon dioxide in a process called "enhanced oil recovery" that injects the gas underground to push out stranded oil reserves. With 80 billion barrels of stranded oil in the U.S.— the equivalent of 14 years of U.S. oil consumption—the prize to figure out a capture-and-delivery solution has grown dramatically.

Geoengineering has as many advocates as critics, who attest that messing with systems that we hardly understand is ill-advised—not to mention that it masks the basic warming problem. The Max Planck Institute for Meteorology in Germany reprogrammed its computer models to estimate the effect proposed space mirrors might have on the planet. The conclusion: substantially lower rainfall in North and South America and northern Europe. Another debate geoengineering has spurred is what happens if the technology falls into the wrong hands. Deep in the World Economic Forum's Global Risks 2013 analysis is a line that paints a scenario "in which a country or small group of countries precipitates an international crisis by moving ahead with deployment or large-scale research independent of the global community. The global climate could, in effect, be hijacked by a rogue country or even a wealthy individual, with unpredictable costs to agriculture, infrastructure and global stability."

The ongoing stalemate regarding mitigation has left some, like Gates, convinced that geoengineering could be humanity's last chance. As Mark Lynas writes in his book *The God Species*, we already have geoengineered a new atmosphere. In fact, the massive impact humans have had on Earth's ecosystems has prompted a movement to declare a new geological epoch. The Holocene is over, according to some scientists. We have entered the Anthropocene, the age of humans. In this era, Lynas argues, we will no longer fight for survival and live at the whim of Mother Nature. Rather, we will re-engineer the planet—and possibly others—to enhance human prosperity.

Ski resorts have been in on the geoengineering game for some time. Vincent Shaefer was the first scientist to make it snow, after discovering in 1946 that dry ice catalyzed crystal formation in a cloud over western Massachusetts's Mount Greylock. Bernard Vonnegut—brother of novelist Kurt—continued the research by using silver iodide, which also induces snowfall when introduced to a cloud. Vail officials say that more than 30 years of seeding have upped snowfall there by 15 percent. Keystone, Breckenridge and Arapahoe Basin recently followed suit, dropping $75,000 each to test five silver iodide cloud-seeding stations.

Snowmaking remains the primary strategy for ski area adaptation—even more so since a few firms achieved the Holy Grail: making snow when it is warm out. Using vacuum technology, IDE Technologies has been producing snow above freezing since the 1990s to cool mines in South Africa. IDE's All Weather Snowmaker now fills in the gap in Zermatt's Theodul Glacier, by turning out 60,000 cubic feet of snow per day—when it's 70 degrees Fahrenheit out. SnowMagic's "Infinite Crystals Snowmaking" uses another method: freezing water in a chamber and delivering snow to the slopes with "controlled and cooled forced air technology." The system can make up to 7,000 cubic feet of dense snow in a 24-hour period. Tennessee's Ober Gatlinburg ski resort in the Great Smoky Mountains installed the system in 2012. That winter, it opened its tubing park earlier than it had in 50 years.

Others in the ski industry are looking beyond snow. Grass skiing has seen a recent resurgence in Europe, China and Japan; and in the UK, more than 60 "dry slope" artificial-surface ski areas see thousands of skiers year-round. There are now 40 snow domes in the world as well, with two dozen others either proposed or under construction. SnowWorld in the Netherlands offers nearly nine acres of slopes and in 2003 became the world's first indoor venue to host an FIS World Cup snowboard race.

Even with climate change, there's likely to be natural snow somewhere on the planet for some time—and developers are eyeing potential venues. Most models project that Siberia and Arctic Canada will see more snow in the next century. Already Russia's prime minister, Dmitry Medvedev, said Russia could expect more than $700 billion by 2025 after developing Siberia as a winter tourism destination. In the spring of 2013 he visited the Sheregesh ski resort, and later Takutsk, to encourage ski area development.

Skiing on grass or in a dome—or even in Siberia, for that matter—might save the business of skiing. But it won't save skiing as we know it, especially powder skiing. Most analysts suggest that if emissions reduction fails, the sport will be practiced by an elite few by 2100 as snow supply shrinks and demand rises. Private clubs like The Yellowstone Club may well be the last bastion of the sport, with expensive snowmaking on the slopes and a few natural flakes in midwinter.

A couple of days after meeting with Paul Julen, the snow came again—real snow, falling out of the sky—and I went skiing with his son, Norbi. It was Easter Sunday and Norbi was guiding a longtime Zermatt guest, Nicholas Paumgarten. Paumgarten is American, though his father was Austrian and he spent much of his early childhood in St. Anton. I refer to him as Mr. P. because he used to raise hell with my mother when they were young and I've known his family since I was a kid.

Mr. P. is 68 years old and has skied Zermatt since 1972. He speaks German with a decent accent and can recite the names of the peaks surrounding the resort from memory. He prefers the Monte Rosa Hotel, where Whymper planned his assault on the Matterhorn, and he gets out on the hill every day no matter the conditions. We met at 9:00 a.m. at the Furi gondola. Norbi told us it was a whiteout up high but that it would clear and we'd have a foot of fresh powder to ourselves. There were hardly any people in line, and those who were peered into the clouds every few minutes, looking for a break. Norbi told us about the local Burgher community, which owns most of the village and the land around it, on the ride up. Like any small town, things get sticky at times, he said, especially when people start talking about no snow in the valley in two generations.

We skied to a chairlift from the gondola, then traversed right from the Furggsattel and headed down one at a time. The snow was light, like Alta light, and we floated down the face in a foot of fresh. The powder billowed around my knees as the pitch fell away. It was effortless, perfect snow, with a foggy haze in the air and the shadows of the Breithorn and Monte Rosa cutting across the valley. We made 40 turns to the bottom and skied straight to the Klein Matterhorn tram.

Mr. P. grinned most of the ride up and didn't say a word. After many decades of skiing, the privilege of a powder day was not lost on him. He lost his father and sister to avalanches and nearly his son and himself to crevasses and ski accidents, yet the high peaks were still clearly his place of renewal. On the next run down Direttissima, he ate up the powder like a fiend, couldn't get enough. It was like it was taking him back, the feeling and the motion of gliding down the mountain conveying him to a time when he was younger and things were different. Not necessarily better, but just different, with the virtue of not knowing what life or the next run would bring.

We rode the Klein Matterhorn again and walked through the tunnel to the slopes slowly. "It's going to clear," Mr. P. said, and it did, a little bit. The Matterhorn's silhouette materialized behind the clouds, followed by the Weisshorn—a prehistoric ring of stony teeth rising up around the valley. The snow was deeper off-piste on skier's left of Klein Matterhorn, hitting my waist and even washing over my head on one turn.

We rode the T-bar across Theodul Pass into Italy next and skied a run at Cervinia. It was sunny over there. The Italians like to tan, so there weren't many people in line and none on the slopes. "They are afraid of the glacier," Norbi said. We skied through boot-top powder above Plan Maison to Gran Somotta, then took the tram to the Rifugio Guide restaurant, where we ate homemade lasagna and drank sodas and waited for it to clear. The sky was misty blue when we emerged and we headed down the Theodul Glacier.

Norbi found powder stashes along the way—500 feet to the left, 300 to the right—then we wrapped right, around to the great white carpet of the Unter Theodul that rolls out from the Breithorn. Deep blue seracs and rockfall interrupted the glacier up high. We skied down the gut, around holes and crevasses. This was the thing that skiers crave: blue sky, cold air, deep snow and miles of it. We didn't stop for 50 turns, then slid into the choke that leads to the foot of the glacier.

Norbi said he remembered when the Theodul and Gorner glaciers met. He said his father remembered stories of grazing cows up here when there were no glaciers at all. "Everything changes," he said. The mandatory rappel off the tongue that used to terrify Mr. P's wife and kids is gone. We skied a tight sluice instead, 100 feet below scars in the rock walls that show where the ice once flowed. A stream trickled through the chasm to a hydroelectric dam. We skied around the water's edge and merged onto a skinny runout. Then we followed Norbi to a trail that led to the valley, where sunlight glinted off the slate roofs and tanning guests of Zermatt.

Chapter Seventeen
The Yellow Brick Road

In the end, to ski is to travel fast and free—free over untouched snow country. To be bound to one slope, even one mountain, by a lift may be convenient but it robs us of the greatest pleasure that skiing can give, that is to travel through the wide wintery country; to follow the lure of peaks which tempt on the horizon and to be alone for a few days or even hours in clear, mysterious surroundings.

—*Hans Gmoser*

If the world ends, the Swiss are heading to Andermatt. The town is set in the middle of a convergence of titanic peaks in south-central Switzerland and was designated as the final fallback of the "Swiss National Redoubt." The Redoubt was a defensive scheme hatched in the 1800s and fine-tuned during the tense years of World War II. It is comprised of a series of fortifications, secret tunnels and bunkers for the Swiss Army in the event of a mass invasion. Warplanes are housed in underground hangars; expansive hospitals are built into mountainsides. After Hitler invaded five surrounding countries in 1940, Swiss soldiers retreated from the Swiss plateau and entrenched in the network of citadels to guard passes leading into Italy. The army's command center was set near St. Gotthard Pass, five miles from Andermatt.[65]

St. Gotthard Pass is the most direct north-south route over the Alps. Napoleon marched his troops over it in 1800 when he invaded Italy. Luminaries like Charles Dickens and William Wordsworth wrote of the danger and dramatic beauty of the gap. In his *Letters from Switzerland* in

1799, Goethe wrote that St. Gotthard "alone has the status of a royal range because it is the point where the largest mountain ranges meet."

Andermatt is the gateway to St. Gotthard and for centuries was a hub of transportation, wealth and power. Until 1882, it was a year-round health resort destination the likes of St. Moritz and Davos. That year, the railroad that put so many Alpine towns on the map wiped Andermatt off it when engineers routed the Gotthard railway tunnel directly *under* the town—effectively turning the road to Andermatt into a dead end.

The military picked up where tourism dropped off, supplying the town with enough jobs, money and infrastructure to get by. But when the great invasion never came, and the Cold War thawed in the early 1990s, the military scaled back. By the time Andermatt's town officials met to discuss the future of the village, many had all but forgotten the 9,721-foot mountain in their backyard down which skiers had been laying tracks since the early 1900s.

Andermatt looked like a ghost town as I cruised through Urseren Valley past rolling green meadows and stands of pine. The mountains were more singular and sheer than in Zermatt—massive piles of rock with twisted ridgelines and wide valleys in between. The jagged summits of Winterstock and Mittagstock greet travelers approaching from the west. Chastelhorn and Gemsstock—the latter, home of the ski area—frame the valley to the south. There are a few trees on the mountainsides, but higher up they are all snow and rock. At its eastern end, the valley runs into Pazolastock Mountain and abruptly stops. Oberalp Pass splits the range there, running up and over to the tiny resort town of Sedrun. To the north, the road to Zurich crosses the infamous Devil's Bridge, which for many years offered sole access to St. Gotthard Pass from the north.

The only sign of the military in Andermatt these days is an infirmary on the north side of town and a few buildings and doorways leading into the mountains. In the village, many of the narrow streets are still cobbled. Hand-hewn chalets are sun-stained, with scalloped bargeboards of the old days. It was dusk when I arrived. I didn't see a soul until I knocked on the door of the Hotel Poste and the night manager meandered across the lobby to open it.

The next day, Benno Nager explained that the quiet nature of the town has been its greatest asset for years. Nager grew up in Andermatt and has witnessed the village transform several times. When he was a kid in the 1960s the ski area was practically abandoned, with just locals, a few hardcore ski mountaineers and powder hippies spinning laps on the tram. In the 1980s the Swedes discovered it, and in the 1990s the big-mountain freeskiing crowd arrived, drawn to the 360 degrees of 5,000-vertical-foot off-piste runs accessed directly off of the tram.

Nager has the look of someone who got into his skiing groove in the 1980s: sunglasses instead of goggles, relaxed vibe, a thick head of brown hair. He spent most of his career at ski resorts in California, where he eventually became Intrawest vice president for development at Mammoth. When Egyptian-born property developer Samih Sawiris proposed one of the largest, most luxurious resorts in the Alps in 2007—smack in the middle of Andermatt—he hired Nager to help him set up the resort-development company and create a master plan for the new ski area, Andermatt-Sedrun.

Sawiris's $2 billion project includes a half dozen luxury hotels, a golf course and more than 500 private apartments and homes—in addition to doubling the size of the ski resort. On the tram ride up Gemsstock, Nager pointed to the massive build site of The Chedi Andermatt, Sawiris's first hotel and apartment complex, then the little town of Sedrun that the ski area will connect to. Above us was the Gurschen Glacier, which runs down the summit of Gemsstock, and to looker's right I could see the St. Anna Glacier and the smaller Winterhorn ski area. In between is the Guspis Valley off-piste area near St. Gotthard Pass, and just out of sight to the left, Nager said, is another hike-to backcountry area "about the size of Vail."

The enormity of the mountain, and the backcountry surrounding it, is best seen from the summit viewing station. The grated metal platform looks back to Zermatt and down into central Switzerland. Crowded in between are two dozen massive mountains with long white aprons, bowls and valleys linking them. You can ski to Italy and back in a day or over to Zermatt, linking the ridges and cirques together. Locals often ride the tram with touring gear and disappear for the rest of the day, if not the week.

We warmed up on a run down the Gurschen from the top. I tried to keep up with Nager's high-speed giant slalom turns down the steep upper third of the glacier, tracking the wave of ice down the slope. Andermatt had a great year in 2012–2013 and the base was soft, packed powder. Nager said it stays untracked for weeks after a storm, and looking at the 200 people we were sharing the mountain with, I understood why.

My quads were burning by the time we stopped a half mile down the slope under the tongue of the glacier. Nager leaned on his poles and told me that the Gurschen used to drop much closer to the valley floor, but that it had receded back to the dogleg we just skied. The glacier lost much of its mass between 1990 and 2005, forcing the resort to build a snow ramp so skiers could get from the summit station to the slope. In 2005, they made an unprecedented move and wrapped more than 30,000 square feet of the upper section of the Gurschen in a synthetic blanket to keep it from melting.

The polyester blanket saved 80 percent of the ice it covered, and now several other resorts use a similar method. The technique was ridiculed by environmentalists as a desperate, shortsighted attempt to stop global warming and save skiing. The thing is, the blanket wasn't installed to save skiing. Like many peaks in the Alps, the summit of Gemsstock is bound together by permafrost, and the glacier keeps much of that ice cold. So if the glacier melts, the permafrost melts, and at some point the top of the mountain is going to fall off—along with the summit station of the tram and everything attached to it.[66]

Andermatt was the last stop on my European tour, and in many ways was the most emblematic of the future of snow and skiing in a warming world. The juxtaposition of the $2 billion development in town, the striking beauty of the valley, the laidback vibe of the locals and the tiny fingernail of a glacier seemingly holding it all together was a microcosm of the fine line that mountain communities are walking.

Melting permafrost is just one of the many side effects of climate change that will likely alter Europeans' lives in the next few decades. In parts of the Alps, the ground is warming at five times the rate of air temperatures. In July 2006, 20 million cubic feet of rock—the size of half of the Empire State Building—broke off the Eiger's east face when permafrost melted. In small Swiss towns like Guttannen in the Bernese Alps, villagers live in fear as frozen ground slowly releases its grip on millions of pounds of rock poised to crash down on them. Other side effects include widespread loss of alpine vegetation and ensuing erosion and landslides. Less snow and early runoff also set the stage for more wildfires, like in the American West, and affect countries like France and Switzerland that depend largely on hydropower.

As far as snow is concerned, most resorts in the Alps did well by the end of the 2012–2013 season—though the pattern of extremes held. The range had its driest fall in 148 years, followed by one of the coldest springs in recent history, which saw blizzards straight through April. The U.S. followed suit, with snow cover slightly above average at 1.4 million square miles.[67] Twenty-six major winter storms crossed the Lower 48 between November and April, and an equally cold spring helped snow totals in Alaska and Western resorts reach average or above. Still, December and January temperatures were well above normal in the contiguous U.S., and the winter ranked as the 20th warmest on record.

Stevens Pass had another banner year, with 193 inches of snow falling in the first 21 days of December. The blizzards kept coming through April, and by the end of the 2012-2013 season the resort had received 501 inches of snow. Stevens logged a record-breaking 400,000 skier visits that year, helping to lighten the shadow cast by the Tunnel Creek tragedy. Despite prognostications that more "thrill-seekers" would be caught in slides in 2013, avalanche deaths across the U.S. dropped by almost 30 percent from 2011–2012.

The deep snow and cold spring of 2013 put climate change skeptics on the offensive, as did a leaked draft of the 2013 IPCC report. The report scaled back the lower end of potential warming from 3.6 degrees Fahrenheit to 2.7 and reduced the probability of global temperatures rising more than 6 degrees Celsius—a minor adjustment considering the devastating impacts that just 3-4 degrees Celsius will have on the planet. Leaked documents revealed confusion among the reports' authors as to how to explain slower warming over the last 15 years. Some of the confusion likely came from the fact that they had explained it many times and there's only a few ways to put it: global warming happens in step changes; the environment absorbs and distributes heat in ways that people don't completely understand; 1998 was unusually warm and not a wise "beginning year" to track any trend. Besides, nine of the warmest years since 1880 have occurred since 1998, and it has indeed continued to warm since then. In an August 2013 special report for *Science*, Noah Diffenbaugh co-authored a study that showed warming is happening 10 times faster than at any time in the last 65 million years—and could very well lead to a 5-6 degrees Celsius rise by the end of the century.

The IPCC report was co-authored by 257 scientists who reviewed 9,200 peer-reviewed studies and two million gigabytes of numerical data. It was the fifth report that the IPCC has released since it was established in 1988. Its importance stems from the fact that it will form the scientific basis for expected U.N. climate change treaty negotiations in 2015. Other findings in the study included a warning regarding the rising pace of melting glaciers. The Arctic ice pack, Greenland ice sheet and Antarctic ice cap all melted faster than estimated in the last study. The report also confirmed that the greatest warming this century will occur mostly during the winter in northern regions.

By the end of 2013, the one thing that everyone from Rex Tillerson of Exxon to German Chancellor Angela Merkel seemed more aligned with was the fact that people are making the planet warmer. And the effects are going to be bad for everyone, no matter their political, philosophical or scientific orientation. The fallout might not mean the end of the world, but it will likely be dangerous for a lot of people. Humanity has become accustomed to certain climactic conditions. The way we feed ourselves, communicate, recreate and survive are related to the climate as well. Which is a sentimental way of saying that everyone in the conversation has the same goal: a safe and prosperous future. As Bill McKibben said, "None of it is easy; there's no yellow brick road. But then the yellow brick road didn't really take you to a wizard, did it? There's only hard work."

Oil and carbon seemed an abstract concept as Nager and I stepped off the tram and skated to the boundary rope. Skiers and tourists mingled around the summit, taking in the view. The air was clear and cold and there was a light breeze. A thin film of cirrus clouds and jet contrails covered the sky, and down in the valley an ominous fog obscured Devil's Bridge.

We ducked the rope and dropped into a crosscut that wrapped around the back side of Gemsstock. Nager stopped at the bottom of a short boot pack, shouldered his skis and trudged up the zigzag path. We took a breather at the top, then traversed into the Guspis, a massive white valley framed by rockbound ridgelines. The snow was wind-scoured at the top, but over the ridge it was boot-top powder. Nager hooted as I dropped in and tracked left, staying high in the shadows on the southwest wall.

We followed the main gut of the canyon beneath Blauberg Peak and St. Gotthard Pass. As it curled to the north into Mätteli, the snow became sun-affected, but hard enough to ski on top of. Nager led the way with 100-foot-long arcs, cruising 35 miles an hour down the fall line. At the bottom we navigated a field of saplings and glided to Route 2, the old road to St. Gotthard Pass. The pavement was covered in several feet of snow, packed down by snowmobiles and skis. I thought about the pilgrims, soldiers and travelers who'd walked this path over the last 1,000 years as we glided down; of the ousted Gaelic Ulster Lord of Ireland, who lost his fortune off Devil's Bridge; and of Charles Dickens, who wrote, "the whole descent between Andermatt…and Altdorf…is the highest sublimation of all you can imagine in the way of Swiss scenery."

We hopped off the road in Hospental, a medieval village built around a watchtower constructed in the 13th century. I followed Nager under the great eaves of the chalets—wooden shutters pinned back, window trim and glaze all perfectly white. I checked out the hand-carved knee brackets, manicured window boxes and scrolled lookout beams as we skied down. It was a different world, from a time before factories, industry and pollution—when people made things with their hands.

Nager stopped to talk to a friend for a moment beside an ancient stone bridge. I wandered around town, unsure of where I was going. I wanted to see it all—absorb the Alpine culture and history and the Swiss way of living close to the mountains and snow. A few chimneys spewed wood smoke into the air, and the ragged lip of the Alps rose above the rooflines. The baroque bulb on top of the Church of Our Lady of the Assumption was patina green, and the slate shingles on an old chalet glowed silver in the afternoon light. Two skiers sat on a bench by the road, and Nager and I joined them. Nager said that he'd called a taxi, and we all waited silently, looking up at the sky, back at Gemsstock, down the road where a few cars whizzed along the Furkastrasse.

Across the street, the pale gray Hotel St. Gotthard shone in the sun. The building was constructed in 1722 and has been a roadhouse ever since. It had been recently redone with a new awning and *Lüftlmalerei* painted around the windows. A gold weathervane jutted from the roof. Back in the day when horses and mules carried people over the pass, the direction of the wind could determine the difference between life and death. Today it indicated that the wind was blowing from the southwest. Low pressure was on the way. Moisture flowing up from the Mediterranean. A big storm was brewing, tonight, maybe tomorrow. Six inches at least. If we're lucky, a foot.

Endnotes

Chapter 2

1   Roland Huntford, *Two Planks and a Passion: The Dramatic History of Skiing* (London: Continuum, 2009 printing), 15-23.

2   John B. Allen, *The Culture and Sport of Skiing—From Antiquity to World War Two* (Amherst: University of Massachusetts Press, 2007), 217–220.

3   Charles J. Sanders, *The Boys of Winter* (Boulder: University Press of Colorado, 2005), 41-58.

4   Seth Masia, "Evolution of Ski Shape," *Skiing History Magazine,* August 29, 2011.

5   Elizabeth Burakowski and Matthew Magnusson, "Climate Impacts on the Winter Tourism Economy in the United States," (Natural Resources Defense Council and Protect Our Winters, 2012).

Chapter 4

6   Warren E. Leary, "NASA Says It Is Time to Build Space Station," *The New York Times*, May 2, 1991.

7   Appy Sluijs, "Subtropical Arctic Ocean Temperatures During the Palaeocene/Eocene Thermal Maximum," *Nature* 441 (June 2006): 610–613.

8   Hal Harvey, Franklin M. Orr, Jr. & Clara Vondrich, "A Trillion Tons," *Dædalus, the Journal of the American Academy of Arts & Sciences*, Winter 2013: 8-22.

9   "Future Climate Change," United States Environmental Protection Agency website, http://www.epa.gov/climatechange/science/future.html.

10 Edward L. Hudgins, "NASA and Mission to Planet Earth" Cato Institute, March 19, 1997, http://www.cato.org/publications/congressional-testimony/nasa-mission-planet-earth.

11 Nalân Koç et al., eds., *Melting Snow and Ice: A Call for Action* (Centre for Ice, Climate and Ecosystems, Norwegian Polar Institute, 2009).

12 Elizabeth Burakowski and Matthew Magnusson, "Climate Impacts on the Winter Tourism Economy in the United States," (Natural Resources Defense Council and Protect Our Winters, 2012), 7.

13 Agrawala, S., "Climate Change in the European Alps: Adapting Winter Tourism and Natural Hazards Management." Organisation for Economic Co-operation and Development, Paris, 2007.

14 John Cook, "Quantifying the Consensus on Anthropogenic Global Warming in the Scientific Literature," *Environmental Research Letters*, 8, (2013): 1-7. Accessed August 2013. doi:10.1088/1748-9326/8/2/024024.

Chapter 6

15 Noah S. Diffenbaugh, Michael A. White, Gregory V. Jones and Moetasim Ashfaq, "Climate adaptation wedges: a case study of premium wine in the western United States," *Environmental Research Letters*, 2011, Volume 6, No. 2.

Chapter 7

16 Mark Moore, Kenny Kramer and Garth Farber, "Northwest Weather and Avalanche Center 2011–2012 Annual Report" (Northwest Weather and Avalanche Center, June 2012).

17 Mark Moore, "Enso and Avalanche Fatalities: Is There a Correlation?" (proceedings of the International Snow Science Workshop, Whistler, British Columbia, September 21–27, 2008).

Chapter 8

18 Daniel Gross, "Going for the Green," *Slate,* February 2010.

19 Elisabeth Rosenthal and Andrew W. Lehren, "Chilling Effect: Carbon Credits Gone Awry Raise Output of Harmful Gas," *The New York Times,* August 9, 2012.

20 "The Global Climate Change Regime," Council on Foreign Relations website, http://www.cfr.org/climate-change/global-climate-change-regime/p21831.

21 Glen P. Peters et. al., "The Challenge to Keep Global Warming Below 2 °C," *Nature Climate Change, 3* (2013), 4.

22 *Turn Down the Heat,* The World Bank (2012), http://climatechange.worldbank.org/sites/default/files/Turn_Down_the_heat_Why_a_4_degree_centrigrade_warmer_world_must_be_avoided.pdf.

Chapter 9

23 S.D. Donner and J. McDaniels, "The Influence of National Temperature Fluctuations on Opinions about Climate Change in the U.S. since 1990," *Climatic Change,* 2013, doi: 10.1007/s10584-012-0690-3.

24 Frederick Mayer, Sarah Adair and Alex Pfaff, "Americans Think the Climate Is Changing and Support Some Action" (Nicholas Institute for Environmental Policy, Duke University).

25 Philip Mote, "Impacts of Climate Variability and Change in the Pacific Northwest" (The JISAO Climate Impacts Group, University of Washington), 20.

26 Steven Saunders, Charles Montgomery and Tom Easley, "Hotter and Drier: The West's Changed Climate" (Natural Resources Defense Council and Rocky Mountain Climate Organization, 2008).

27 Seth Borenstein, "Climate Contradiction: Less Snow, More Blizzards," Associated Press website, February 18, 2013, accessed August 2013, http://bigstory.ap.org/article/climate-contradiction-less-snow-more-blizzards.

28 "Overview of the Millennium Ecosystem Assessment," United Nations Environment Programme website, http://www.unep.org/maweb/en/About.aspx.

29 "National Overview: Annual 2012" (National Oceanic and Atmospheric Administration, January 8, 2013), http://www.ncdc.noaa.gov/sotc/national/2012/13.

Chapter 10

30 Peter H. Hansen, *The Summits of Modern Man: Mountaineering after the Enlightenment*, (Cambridge: Harvard University Press, 2013).

31 Alen Weber, *Because It's There: A Celebration of Mountaineering from 200 B.C. to Today* (Boulder: Taylor Trade Publications, 2003).

32 Trevor Braham, *When the Alps Cast Their Spell: Mountaineers of the Golden Alpine Age* (Scotland: Neil Wilson Ltd., 2005).

33 Francis Henry Gribble, *The Early Mountaineers* (T.F. Unwin, 1899).

34 Luc Moreau, "The Mer de Glace, A Lively Glacier," (2012, Compagnie du Mont-Blanc).

35 Shardul Agrawala, "Climate Change in the European Alps: Adapting Winter Tourism and Natural Hazards Management," Organization for Economic Co-operation and Development, January 2007.

36 Erla Zwingle, "Meltdown: The Alps Under Pressure," *National Geographic*, November 2009, accessed August 2013.

37 Rolf Bürki, Hans Elsasser and Bruno Abegg, "Climate Change and Winter Sports: Environmental and Economic Threats," University of Zurich, December 2, 2003.

Chapter 11

38 Mark Lynas, *The God Species* (National Geographic, 2011).

39 Brian Handwerk, "Little Ice Age Shrank Europeans, Sparked Wars," *National Geographic,* October 3, 2011.

40 "World of Change," NASA.gov, http://earthobservatory.nasa.gov/Features/WorldOfChange/decadaltemp.php.

41 Luc Moreau, "The Mer de Glace, A Lively Glacier" (Compagnie du Mont-Blanc, 2013).

42 Kim Willsher, "A Glorious Winter, but the Alps Face a Warmer World – Bringing Huge Change," *The Guardian*, March 13, 2013.

Chapter 12

43 Alexandra Liebing, ed., *Climate Change in the Alps* (Federal Ministry for the Environment and Nature Conservation and Nuclear Safety, Berlin: 2007), 17-18.

44 Julienne C. Stroeve et. al, "The Arctic's rapidly shrinking sea ice cover: a research synthesis," National Snow and Ice Data Center, *Climatic Change,* June 2011, DOI 10.1007/s10584-011-0101-1.

45 Carolyn Pumphrey "Global Climate Change: National Security Implications," Strategic Studies Institute, May 2008, http://www.strategicstudiesinstitute.army.mil/pdffiles/pub862.pdf.

Chapter 13

46 Alexandra Liebing, ed., *Climate Change in the Alps (*Federal Ministry for the Environment and Nature Conservation and Nuclear Safety, Berlin: 2007), 11.

47 Agrawala, S., "Climate Change in the European Alps: Adapting Winter Tourism and Natural Hazards Management." Organisation for Economic Co-operation and Development, Paris, 2007.

48 Alexandra Liebing, ed., *Climate Change in the Alps* (Federal Ministry for the Environment and Nature Conservation and Nuclear Safety, Berlin, 2007).

49 Tim Appenzeller, "The Case of the Missing Carbon," NationalGeographic.com, accessed September 2013, http:// environment.nationalgeographic.com/environment/ global-warming/missing-carbon/#page=2.

50 "Satellites See Unprecedented Greenland Ice Sheet Surface Melt," NASA.gov, last modified July 24, 2012, http://www.nasa.gov/ topics/earth/features/greenland-melt.html.

51 *Turn Down the Heat* (The World Bank, 2012), http://climatechange. worldbank.org/sites/default/files/Turn_Down_the_heat_ Why_a_4_degree_centrigrade_warmer_world_must_be_avoided.pdf.

52 "How Much More Will Earth Warm?," NASA.gov, accessed September 2013, http://earthobservatory.nasa.gov/Features/ GlobalWarming/page5.php.

Chapter 14

53 Bill McKibben, "Global Warming's Terrifying New Math," *Rolling Stone*, July 19, 2012.

54 "Carbon Emissions Per Person, By Country," *The Guardian,* accessed September 2013, http://www. theguardian.com/ environment/datablog/2009/sep/02/carbon-emissions-per- person-capita?guni=Data:in%20body%20link.

55 Wolfgang Knorr, "Is the Airborne Fraction of Anthropogenic Carbon Dioxide Increasing?," *Geophysical Research Letters*, November 2009, http://onlinelibrary.wiley.com/doi/10.1029/2009GL040613/abstract, DOI: 10.1029/2009GL040613.

56 "Can China Clean Up Fast Enough?," *The Economist*, August 10, 2013.

57 Quirin Schiermeier, "How Soot Killed the Little Ice Age," Nature.com, September 2, 2013, accessed September 2013, http://www.nature.com/news/how-soot-killed-the-little-ice-age-1.13650.

58 John B. Allen, *The Culture and Sport of Skiing: From Antiquity to World War Two* (Amherst: University of Massachusetts Press, 2007), 77–80.

59 Bettina Menne, Franklin Apfel, Sari Kovats and Francesca Racioppi, eds., "Protecting Health in Europe From Climate Change" (World Health Organization, 2008).

60 *Turn Down the Heat* (The World Bank, 2012), http://climatechange.worldbank.org/sites/default/files/Turn_Down_the_heat_Why_a_4_degree_centrigrade_warmer_world_must_be_avoided.pdf.

Chapter 15

61 Robert Steiger and Johann Stötter, "Climate Change Impact Assessment of Ski Tourism in Tyrol," (Tourism Geographies: *An International Journal of Tourism Space, Place and Environment* (2013): 1, accessed September 2013, doi: 10.1080/14616688.2012.762539.

62 Lester R. Brown, "World on the Edge: How to Prevent Environmental and Economic Collapse," Earth Policy Institute website, accessed September 2013, http://www.earth-policy.org/books/wote/wotech8.

Chapter 16

63 Hansruedi Müller and Fabian Weber, "Climate Change and Tourism: Scenario Analysis for the Bernese Oberland in 2030," *Tourism Review 63*, no. 3: 57–71.

64 Marc Gunther, "The Business of Cooling the Planet," *Fortune* on CNN, October 7, 2011, accessed September 2013, http://tech.fortune.cnn.com/2011/10/07/the-business-of-cooling-the-planet.

65 "Swiss Reveal Secret World: Their Defense from Nazis," *The New York Times*, July 25, 1999.

66 Dr. Marcia Phillips, "Snow, Glaciers and Permafrost," Institute for Snow and Avalanche Research, SLF, accessed September 2013, http://www.congresdeneu.ad/historic/08-marcia-phillips.pdf.

67 "National Overview—January 2013," National Climatic Data Center website, accessed September 2013, http://www.ncdc.noaa.gov/sotc/national/2013/.